After the Pain

Transforming Pain into Personal Power

LaChish Latimer

Heather,

Thank you for your support in this process. It's been a pleasure working with you. I enjoy our talks about family, marriage, & God. You inspire me balancing life, work, motherhood, & being a wife.

Love
LaChish Latimer

FOREWORD

LaChish (McClurkin) Latimer and I had the privilege of building the Kingdom of God at Camp Casey, Korea back in 2003, serving in the United States Army. The first time I met her, she radiated a spirit of Godliness, which is rare among soldiers. Immediately, her calling was evident, and it was strikingly obvious the hand of God was moving in her life. A few months ago, Lachish contacted me to review her book, and to write a foreword. It is an honor to introduce you to her work. "After the Pain: Transforming Pain Into Personal Power" is a compelling account of personal pain, and persistence. Lachish does a masterful job walking the reader through her account of past pain and present triumph. I was not the least bit surprised as the words graphically came to life on each page. She is a guide, whose navigation takes the reader from pain to the shores of healing, which I found most refreshing. Lachish is not afraid to take the reader deep into her world, exposing past vulnerabilities and struggles. She invites us to travel with her through the traumatic experience of child birth, childhood, and broken self-esteem. This book is more than a story of lessons learned, it represents a collaboration of life's pain and life's ultimate joy, which is birthed through the process of pain. I invite you to travel through the valley of the shadow of death with Lachish, knowing that in spite of the mountainous terrain, the Good Shepherd is with you guiding your every move.

Chaplain (LTC) Eddie Kinley, Jr.

Unites States Army

LaChish Latimer

TABLE OF CONTENTS

Acknowledgements

From the Author

ACKNOWLEDGMENTS

I want to acknowledge my parents. My mother, Marsheila D. Sowell, who taught me more lessons than she intended. She is certainly one of the hardest working women I know, with one of the biggest hearts of gold. And my father, Irc J. McClurkin, who has been a constant supporter of every dream I've ever had. This man developed me into a princess through his unfailing love and always held me to a high standard. My step-mother, Debra McClurkin, showed women could have a voice in ministry and instilled in me that my lifestyle was more important than any sermon I could preach.

I thank God for my siblings: Davida Johnson, Larry Johnson, Iric McClurkin, Faith Johnson, and Michelle Marshall. Special thanks to Iric because he has inspired me to write this book through his heart of forgiveness. Many times when I didn't want to forgive, my big brother always encouraged me to give people another chance. Although he doesn't preach in public, he ministers to me one on one through my hardest seasons.

My children, Judah and Zion Latimer, give me the courage and wings to take flight! Whenever I want to doubt what I can do, their beautiful eyes and smiles give me faith to conquer anything. To Mr. Daniel Latimer Sr., for blessing me with the gift of motherhood and encouraging me to go after and use every gift and talent bestowed upon me.

Thanks to my personal team for editing and review: Tracie Dixon-Stanley, Andrew Smith III, & Eddie Kinley. To my styling and photography team: Sammie Haynes, Nathan Pearcy, Deeonna Sharnay, & Lakisha Beauford.

Special thanks to everyone God has used as an instrument to sharpen me, whether through support or conflict. All of you have helped to mold me and impart this wisdom I am sharing with the world. Finally, thank you for purchasing and reading this book!

Simply LaChish

From the Author

I've been a writer since I was a child. I would write poetry as a therapeutic outlet for the things in life that were overwhelming. I would write from my soul and receive such a peace after dumping my weights onto the paper. I'm grateful to God for the gift of writing in many forms and also grateful to the people who have encouraged and helped nurture my gift.

As you prepare to read the content of this book, I must warn you that transparency is a huge part of my teaching style. While watching an interview of Maya Angelou she said something that really resonated in my spirit. It was very simple, but powerful. She said, "When you get, give. When you learn, teach." At times, I've been reluctant to share what I've learned for fear I had not learned enough to share anything significant. But as I really began to inventory the various situations I've experienced, I could see the classroom God placed me in.

Some people call me an "old soul," or say "you're mature beyond your years." I don't know that I completely agree with those statements, however, what I do know is that in my years I've experienced some intense situations that forced me to seek understanding sooner. I refused to be placed in the same tests because I kept failing. So I set out to learn the lesson God knew I needed. One of the biggest lessons I've had to learn, and am yet learning, is how to forgive quickly and heal from painful experiences.

Every human will experience pain at many junctions in life. However, the perception used to analyze that pain will determine whether it helps make you stronger, or weakens the fabric of your heart, mind, and soul. My goal is to share an effective pathway that turns every painful experience into fuel and strength to become even greater than you were prior to when the pain began.

Forgiveness is one of the requirements for a Christian to be forgiven of their trespasses from God. However, forgiveness is not always an easy process, especially when you've been offended or hurt multiple times by the same person. I used to hold grudges like no other. You only had to cross me once and you would be cut off for months, years, and maybe even a lifetime depending on the extent of the pain caused. I tried at one time to forgive while not allowing the person to forget they've offended me. I was not able to continue in a relationship on the same level after being hurt. I didn't care who it was, family, friends, co-workers, church people, strangers, whoever.

While I felt like cutting people off was the solution, I later found that although I was no longer interacting with that person, the grudge was keeping them closer to me than I thought. I have found this truth to be very enlightening, when you do not forgive the hurt caused to you, you give space to reproduce that same hurt from you. This is how people become the very things they hate.

Take this journey with me as we uncover the hurts that

may have been swept under the rug, but have greatly affected your choices subconsciously and sometimes consciously. There is liberty when you learn to transform pain into personal strength.

www.Simply LaChish.com

LaChish Latimer

1

The Pain

DELIVERY PAIN

On the night of December 8, 2014 I went into labor with my second son, Zion. Just a day prior I started irregular contractions and went into the labor and delivery unit to be evaluated. I was anxious to deliver this little boy. The nurse sent me home and said not to come back until my contractions were 5-10 minutes apart for at least an hour. So at 10 p.m. on the 8th I went to lie down on and by eleven the labor pains began. They were every ten to fifteen minutes, lasting about five to ten seconds each time. I knew this was "IT!" However, I waited at home while my oldest son and husband slept. The later it got, the more intense my pain grew, yet I was waiting for the contractions to become more frequent. Needless to say I didn't get any rest at all that night.

Finally, at 5 a.m. I went to the restroom and noticed the "bloody show." That's when I woke my husband up and began preparing to go to the hospital. After dropping Judah off with a baby sitter, we headed straight to the hospital. When I checked in the nurses were preparing for change of shift. Being a nurse I knew this meant I wouldn't be seen for a little while because the night shift was leaving, and the day shift would need to get settled in first. An hour later I met my nurse and was hooked up to the baby monitor and physically assessed.

I was hurting at that time, but I was mentally prepared for the lightning bolt contractions. I would breathe my way through them and relax in between. I remember the nurse asking me how bad the pain was on a scale of 0-10. I said around a 7, however, she didn't believe me because I was too calm. That would be the beginning of the horror. I texted my inner circle that I was in labor and maybe I should just cry so the staff would understand how much pain I was bearing. Too bad I'm not a crier when it comes to physical pain.

Two hours later the nurse checked me again and I was 4 cm dilated and 90% effaced. Finally, they agreed I was in active labor and began drawing labs and starting my IV. By now the contractions were worse and more frequent, but I was still "maintaining" my composure. The staff was in no rush, by now I was asking for pain medicine and epidural.

Unfortunately, my labs weren't sent down immediately, so there was a delay in calling anesthesia for my epidural. When the anesthesiologist entered the room I was in EXTREME pain! By now I was climbing out of the bed with each contraction, and the contractions seemed to never stop, simply going from bad to worse, then back to bad. The nurse was instructing me to breathe through it, stay calm, and stay in the bed! That's one of the first moments I knew I was really saved, because I didn't curse her out or become rude. By this time my husband was walking in and out of the room because he couldn't handle seeing me in that much pain.

The anesthesiologist tried to position me for the epidural. There I was sitting on the side of the bed trying to be as still as possible while I felt like I was being electrocuted. It was a piece of cake! A very dry, disgusting piece of cake. As I tried to cooperate, the anesthesiologist began to say I was very small and he couldn't get in the space in my back to place the epidural. For at least thirty minutes he stuck me multiple times and never made a successful placement.

At this time I was getting very frustrated and again I said to myself, "I know I'm saved!" All I could do was begin to pray, "God, help me!" Suddenly, a contraction hit and I began to bear down against my will. Fluids were gushing so I asked the nurse, "What's going on? Where is all this coming from?" She insisted I stop pushing and lay down. I couldn't lay down. I couldn't be still. I couldn't follow her instructions. In my mind, she was standing there pain free, and I was having the worse pain of my life, what did she know? The next contraction hit and I yelled and felt my body pushing again. At this time I lost control of my urinary and bowel functions. Some kind of way, I laid down long enough to be checked and Zion's head was crowning.

Whoa! I went from being 4 cm before anesthesiologist arrived to within an hour my baby was coming out regardless of my pain management. I asked the nurse, "Can't you give me something for pain?" Her response was somewhat cynical. She said, "Ma'am, the baby is coming right now. There's no time." Yes, this was the third time I knew I had Jesus in my heart and the Holy Spirit keeping my tongue. I'd been there three hours without receiving a drop of pain medicine, even after telling them how badly I was hurting.

By now the room was full of rushing nurses and doctors begging me not to push at all because they needed everyone in place before the baby arrived. In a matter of minutes my room was flooded with both teams, the infant team and mommy team. Now they were ready for me to push. I took a deep breath and pushed long and hard. Zion was coming through the birthing canal and I felt every single movement. They asked me to stop and push once more and in a blink of an eye, Zion came sliding out.

Everyone in the room was full of excitement and emotion…everyone except me. My husband stood there crying and trying to explain how proud he was of me. He was telling me how amazing I was and did and just all excited. And I just laid there angry because these people just made one of the most joyous of occasions miserable for me.

By now my body was shaking uncontrollably. Someone said, "She's cold." But I wasn't cold, I was hurting. The OBGYN began trying to suture and repair my tears. Apparently the nurse forgot to tell him I never got my epidural. I could feel every needle poke and finger pressing on my very tender body. The doctor quickly apologized and asked for a local anesthetic so he could finish his job without hurting me too bad. It still hurt.

I just laid there looking at the ceiling. I sent my husband to go check on the baby. I was hurting so bad I didn't want to even hold my baby yet. An hour after delivery I got my first pain pill. While the oral pain medicine was trying to work I had an intravenous medication causing more contractions to slow my bleeding, which caused more pain. After another hour the IV medication was complete and the oral medication was finally kicking in. Roughly two hours after delivery I was finally ready to see and hold my baby.

I have to be honest, I was mad at that little boy. I was mad at everyone on the staff too! But as I continued to hold him and look at him, the pain didn't go away magically, but the anger did. After all, he wasn't to blame for my pain. Zion didn't intend to hurt me. He had no idea what was going on. All he wanted to do was sleep. The delivery process had been rough on him too. I can look back and smile now, but it was no laughing matter then.

It took me weeks to move without pain. There was pain from the delivery process. There was pain from the epidural attempts. There was pain from my body trying to adjust back to the right size and function after the baby was out. There was pain from my breasts preparing to feed and nourish the baby. The doctor gave me instructions to rest and recover for six weeks before my follow up appointment. After the six weeks he told me to ease back slowly into my physical exercise regimen.

THE PAIN

The Dictionary definition of pain is "physical suffering or distress, as due to injury, illness, etc.; a distressing sensation in a particular part of the body; mental or emotional suffering or torment."

In the medical field we say "pain is subjective." When we ask a client how they rate their pain on a scale of 0-10, 0 being no pain, 10 being the worse pain they could ever imagine, we understand that a 2 out of 10 for one person could very well be a 10 out of 10 for another person. The patient rates the pain based on their tolerance and ability to endure the pain they are experiencing. Some people have a higher tolerance for pain, while others have seemingly no tolerance for pain. As I've worked at the bedside of many patients immediately after surgery one thing has become evident to me, a patient's tolerance for the pain they feel currently is directly affected by their past experiences of pain. For someone who has never had severe pain, mild or moderate procedures could be considered the most severe pain ever. However, for patients who have had severe experiences with pain, i.e. burn victims, broken bones, high impact collisions, etc., they tend to rate every other pain much lower than the average person.

THE WORSE PAIN

After saying all of that, the delivery pain with Zion was the worse physical pain I'd ever experienced. Next to that I would say the headache I suffered while having viral meningitis. Yet both of these unbearable physical pains could never compare to the depth of an emotional or mental blow.

As a person who stands before people as a leader, both professionally, socially, and spiritually, I often find myself in a position where I have to put my emotional conditions to the side to focus on the mission. I've heard preachers say things like, "preaching while bleeding," or "leading while bleeding." It happens all too often with people who have dependents, meaning those who pull on their strength or the image of their strength. Those seeking advice, wisdom, and direction who have submitted or subjected themselves to the wisdom, experience, and knowledge of a person perceived to be more advanced than themselves in specific areas.

While it is a privilege to be considered for such a great role, it can also be a crippling position when overwhelmed by the pressures of appearing to be strong at all times. I've found the worse pain to be the pain you can't admit you're in while you're hurting.

Many of us can admit and seek medication or treatment for physical pain. However, emotional and mental pain is often left untreated and unresolved. This is especially true in people who have correlated pain with weakness. To admit that you've actually been hurt in your soul can be a frightening truth to face, but it is a reality everyone must face.

There are so many sources of pain in this world. We can be hurt through disappointments, betrayals, failures, lies, abandonment, abuse, taunting, teasing, critical comments, rejection, and much more.

AGENTS OF PAIN

OTHER PEOPLE: In my life I've experienced a variety of painful situations. When I reflect on pain brought on by people I've trusted, loved, believed in, or sacrificed for, it made it hard for me to forgive them, and certainly even harder to allow them to stay in my heart. It used to be said of me, "LaChish can hold a grudge." What people didn't realize about me was it really took a lot to get me to that place. I never was angered easily, or hurt by simple things. Whenever I allowed someone access to my introverted heart, it was a huge deal for me that they took care of their special invitation to my most sacred space.

One of the earliest pains I can remember occurred when my parents separated. While they had never been married, as a preschooler I didn't know the difference. All I knew was mommy and daddy lived in the same house. This was so long ago I can't remember all the details. Quite frankly many of the details are not my story to tell. What I can say is even as a small child I was disappointed that I wouldn't grow up in a home with both my parents present. Thankfully I had a father who would be great to me regardless of not being a live-in dad. Yet I was hurt because I felt like I deserved the best. In my mind the best was both parents living together to raise their children. From that pain I made a vow to myself early in life that I would not have sexual intercourse until I was married, because I did not want to get pregnant by a man who was not my husband and who would not guarantee that my children grew up in a home with both parents present.

That hurt, left unresolved, placed unrealistic ideals and goals in my heart and mind. It was not unrealistic to wait until I was married to share myself with a man and become a mother. It was unrealistic to believe it would be that simple. I had a whole list of things I did not want in a potential spouse, and that I did not want to become or repeat. All of these things stemmed from an unresolved hurt I had as a little girl. Sadly enough, when little girl hurt meets grown woman, a war is bound to break loose. I became many things I said I wouldn't. I repeated poor behaviors I said I wouldn't. I made decisions I said I wouldn't. I've finally learned why, and it's because I did not deal with the pain properly.

I was hurt by my mother because I did not understand why she kicked my father out. I was hurt by my father because I did not understand why he did things that caused her to kick him out. I was mad at both of them because I couldn't understand why they provoked each other to act in ugly and unattractive ways, which lead to the demise of it all. I was, above all the anger, hurt because I felt like they made selfish decisions without considering my brother and I. That was my childhood impression, and that was my pain from home.

Another life changing and painful event was when I was introduced to sexual contact through the touching of private parts and grinding with clothes on. I was probably six or seven years old when another child, although much older than myself, would open up the door for sexual perversion. The ugly word of molestation comes to fruition in hindsight. Nonetheless, I was first angry with others around I felt should have sheltered and "saved me" from this exposure. It was not an incident that occurred deep in some secret place. Sadly, because others were enjoying themselves, no one took time to notice that I was not excited for the activities.

It took several years for me to realize what had taken place and what it really meant. It only took a moment for the pain to make an impression on my heart and mind and emotional state. Like many others, I continued to participate in inappropriate situations because an appetite had been awakened in me that I was not mentally mature enough to handle. While people think kids don't go through much, or see much, this is the furthest thing from truth. Before I was ten I knew what it meant for girls to "like" girls and touch one another. I knew what it was like for people who were related to kiss and grind and dig in each other's clothes. I'd seen pornographic images. I knew what male private parts looked like. I didn't want to know. I seemingly couldn't avoid it. I was hurt because the first time I didn't feel like I had any control, but the other times I wanted to feel some control. At the end of the day, and end of that period of my life, I can honestly look back and say not only did I feel pain, but potentially became an agent to cause pain.

The idea that I could cause pain or disappointment to others was a depressing one. I battled with depression beginning as early as the fourth grade. I'd seen and participated in things I couldn't make peace with. I didn't want to be a whore, or homosexual, or promiscuous. I wanted to be normal. I wanted to be a good child. I wanted to be a special child. The pressure of being perfect was in my nature very early in life. This mental pressure and pain was overwhelming. My first attempt at suicide was when I was only nine years old. That pain was far worse than any labor pain I could ever experience. The pain of needing help and not having a peace to ask for it was one I don't want to remember, but can barely forget.

I can remember attempting suicide together with my brother Iric. We were both so young, but found ourselves ready to quit on life. We were on welfare. We didn't have the hottest clothes or shoes. We went to the store with food stamps. We lived in a neighborhood where shooting, drugs, gangs, and poverty were the norm. One day we both decided we were ready to check out. We got two of my jump ropes and proceeded to hang ourselves off the banister. Can you imagine the impact this would have had on my mother? Coming home from work and finding both her children dead over the stairwell? We were not at all concerned with how anyone else would feel. We had tunneled vision and we went for it. I'm alive today because one of the ropes broke. I can remember thinking, "if we both don't go, neither of us can."

Painful impressions continued throughout my youth and into adulthood. Too many situations to describe in detail. In short, I've been choked and told "I will kill you" by two different people in my life I trusted to love me unconditionally. I've been betrayed multiple times by friends and companions through infidelity, backstabbing, abandonment, and simply shifts in loyalty. I know what it's like to be told to my face "You will never be anything," "You're stupid," "You're ugly." I know that my nose is big, my skin is dark, my lips are big, and my body petite. My breasts and hips are not "big enough," and I went from being mislabeled a "freak and gay", to then being told "I wasn't enough of a freak" and "being too holy." I understand how it feels to be laughed at when sharing my hopes and dreams. I remember being dogged for my failures and ostracized for my mistakes. The people who have meant the most to me have been responsible for the greatest pains of my life, along with the greatest joys of course.

As long as you are alive and breathing and existing in the presence of other people, people are bound to at one time or another cause pain to enter your life. I've learned to simply accept that as a fact of life. And with that fact, I also understand and am very conscious of the fact that I too will cause pain to others. Although I try not to intentionally hurt anyone, I have learned that a person's perception far outweighs your intentions. So we can settle the case and all agree, people will continue to make decisions, comments, or actions that will not be received with joy by everyone connected to them, thus causing pain.

GOD: While many thoughts have come to your mind while reading thus far of the many people who have caused you pain or discomfort in your life, there is another agent of pain I've experienced...GOD! Oh what great pains I've felt in this little heart at the hands of God! Don't get alarmed, I'm sure you've felt some of these same pains in your life, or have the potential to feel them in the future.

The first of my GOD pains that comes to mind are "unanswered prayers." A better truth would be, prayers that were not answered the way I wanted them to be have been painful. Praying for God to heal loved ones who were sick and dying, and they died anyway. That was painful. When you apply your faith, fast and pray, and commit yourself to believing God for miracles you never get, it is painful.

Various times I've put situations in God's hands and trusted Him, and found myself disappointed. Sometimes disappointed because I felt He should've changed certain people, or prevented them from hurting me. Sometimes disappointed because I tried my hardest at things, believing God for success and failed. Sometimes disappointed because His will didn't line up with mine. Nevertheless, I have had disappointments in this Christian walk, and disappointment is also painful.

Because I know God is in control and omnipotent, I have felt hurt when He did not use His power to prevent tragedies, perform miracles, or rescue me from situations in the way I felt was best. Obviously I know God does not need my advice, nor suggestions, or educated guesses to help Him direct my path. Even understanding God is not my genie in a bottle, or Santa Clause, or wishing well, the human part of me still gets disappointed and my feelings still get hurt with God's perfect plan.

Some argue there must not be a God because if there was such a being with all power who is perfect, full of love and wisdom, then why is the world the way it is? They use the fact that God does not always intervene in the affairs of men as an excuse to say He does not exist. These people are disappointed because God hasn't made the world perfect. He allows pain to exist. This truth has caused some so much anguish that they reject God altogether.

YOURSELF: The biggest agent of pain in my life has been ME! While I can tell various stories of all the things people have done to me, and what God didn't do for me, my own list of self-inflicted pains far outweigh all of that.

There are very few people I know who purposely hurt themselves. However, there are people who get a thrill out of self-inflicted pain, and those people I do not claim to understand. I am not one of those people who enjoys pain, nor invites painful situations to my life with a smile or a hug. Yet I have made some unwise decisions, whether out of emotions, impulse, or ignorance. I have picked the wrong people to keep close to my heart, subjected myself to abusive situations, put pressure and stress on myself far beyond what was mentally healthy. I have been my biggest critic, and many times worst supporter.

By far the worse pain I could ever cause myself, is the pain felt by harboring unforgiveness in my heart. Allowing myself to become bitter, resentful, and even going as far as hating people did more internal damage than anyone else could do. I was miserable long after the other person had moved on happily in life. I was restricted to a life without joy, peace, and contentment because I refused to move on from the day I was hurt. I was succeeding in one area, while decaying in another. Even when I accomplished great things I could not be genuinely happy or proud of myself.

I've tried to kill me more than anyone else ever could. I've tried to kill myself with low self-esteem. I beat myself down mentally over what I didn't like in the mirror. I beat myself down over what I couldn't achieve on my first attempt. I held myself to a standard of perfection that was never meant to be a measuring rod. If I made a mistake, I was my own judge and jury and my sentence was always death and hell. I've tried to kill myself emotionally by not allowing myself to feel. I worked hard at being numb, staying composed, and appearing healthy to others. I tortured myself, imploding while being the picture of a modeled woman before the masses.

I damaged myself by not allowing me to be honest with me! Making myself lie to myself so that I could keep up lying to others. I hurt myself trying to be like others and not allowing myself to just be me. The voice in my head has been far more influential than the voice of anyone else. I'm willing to take that responsibility and own the pain I've caused myself.

As we move forward in this book, I want to help you: acknowledge and identify your pains; forgive the source that caused the pain; heal from the hurt of that pain; and transform that pain into a productive experience that bears good fruit in your life. It doesn't matter who has caused the pain. What matters is how you handle that pain.

2

Processing the Pain

HILL TRAINING

My freshman year at Central High School in Philadelphia, I went out for the cross-country team. Even on the day of try outs, I didn't know what cross-country really was. I knew that I liked to run, and I just assumed we were a track team that traveled more.

I didn't realize we would run through natural terrain, up and down hills, and in and out of wooded areas. The first day they took us on a one loop lap. It was approximately 1.3 miles. When we started the run I remember thinking to myself, "this is a really slow track team." I obviously didn't know the distance we were going to run. Most city blocks are not 1.3 miles around. It didn't take long for people to start falling behind on this "slow short run." I was maintaining pretty good until about halfway through, then I began to feel winded. Soon after that we began running up a steep hill. On the hill I went from a shuffle, to a brisk walk, to a walk, to a walk with heavy breathing, to wanting to just stand still and catch my breathe.

I can laugh at that first practice day now because I would go on to run cross-country all four years of high school and even walk on to the Columbus State University of Columbus, GA cross-country team and become a scholarship athlete. I grew to love cross-country. I remember in college running 10-12 miles every Sunday morning during the season as our longest days, and our "short runs" were no less than thirty minutes, usually between 3-4 miles.

I found out I wasn't a good track runner in high school after my first great season of cross-country running. I earned a championship varsity jacket my first three years of high school, although my senior year we did not win, I was still one of the top seven runners. The first problem, I wasn't very quick. My strength was being an endurance runner. On the track, however, I found it boring running in a circle for 8 laps as a two mile runner. I tried the one mile race and just found there were quicker people. I couldn't understand how the people I crushed during cross-country season were crushing me during track season.

Finally it clicked! I was stronger running hills. In high school after each practice we were supposed to run hills. We had a steep hill right behind the school that was good for training. So I built my strength and endurance working on that hill. During the cross-country races I always passed my runners going up the hill. I never wanted to leave it to chance for a sprint at the end on flat ground because that was too even for my opponent. I learned to physically and mentally beat my challengers going up the hill.

There is a saying among athletes that "pain is weakness leaving the body." Both my high school and college coaches had one very big thing in common, they both believed practice should hurt worse than any race day. I learned how to process the pain of practice so that it worked in my benefit for race days. While others didn't want to give 100% in practice and slacked on their hill training, I was giving it all I had. I knew when all eyes were on me in a race I wanted to be prepared to win.

I learned to embrace being sore after practices, especially in the beginning of the season. I understood that as I ripped my muscles in training, they would heal stronger and larger. The pain in practice became my measuring rod for how effective I was in preparation.

The heart and mind of a true champion understands that there is a process to victory. It begins with embracing and perceiving the pain as a means to greatness.

PERCEPTION IS REALITY

If anyone discovers a way to live in this world with no pain, please let me know how. We will all undoubtedly experience pain in all forms: physical, mental, and emotional. The severity of the pain will vary and the frequency of the experience of pain may as well. Yet the fact remains we can expect to some experience pain by uncontrollable, and sometimes preventable circumstances. What I've learned matters more is how we perceive and process that experience.

In the military we are obligated to go through resiliency training. The purpose of this training is to teach soldiers how to mentally process various stressful situations so that we are not overwhelmed, depressed, full of anger, or mentally suffering. Every three months we must go through a module of training. One of the first lessons I recall deals with perception. You must first identify an activating event, something that happens which could potentiate a negative thought or emotion in you.

For example, when you are driving and a car cuts you off is an activating event. You have to address the first thought that comes to your mind. Do you think to yourself, "Wow, I hope that other driver is okay"? More of us think, "What's wrong with you!?!" and proceed to calling them names of our choice. It is a normal response to be agitated by someone potentially putting you in danger by driving recklessly. What is not normal is allowing that event to ruin your entire day or week.

One could argue this situation is more of a frustrating event as opposed to a painful one. Perhaps a better example is coming home one day after losing your job and having your spouse walk out and leave you. The first thought could be, "Life as I know it is officially over!" That may very well be the case. Whether that's a completely negative thing or not depends on your perception.

Walking into a room to you find your spouse in the bed with another person is without question a painful activating event. The response taken in those critical moments makes a world of difference. Some see red, snap, and end up on trial for murder. Others may end up with assault charges. Another may kick both people out of the house naked and embarrass them. Still others may turn around and walk out. It's all the same situation with various responses. The key to their response is their perception. The first two responses are to take justice into their own hands and repay them for such disrespect. The third response wants revenge but doesn't want permanent repercussions from criminal charges. The last is likely afraid of responding like the first two and walks away because they don't know how far they'll actually go.

Another painful scenario that is handled differently based on perception is a miscarriage. Some take it as a punishment from God. Others find themselves feeling guilty because they couldn't carry their child full term.

Some respond by immediately trying for a child again. Other become fearful and hesitantly try again after waiting for a period of time. Others become fearful and never try again. Everyone is affected by the situation. The extent of its effects is dependent upon their perception of the reason this event occurred.

More personally, when I was sixteen years old I went on a mission trip to Kenya, Africa. At the end of the two week mission I became ill. It started with fevers and abdominal pain. I was actually restricted to the physician's home, the deacon physician we were there supporting. When I returned to the United States I was still very uncomfortable. Then a new symptom began, I started bleeding. At first I thought I was menstruating, but it continued for twelve days!!!

I ended up going to the hospital. They couldn't find the cause. I had referrals for specialist to check my kidneys. Those results came back fine. I went to a gastrointestinal specialist. Those results were fine too. No doctor could find the source of my illness.

Here I was, entering my senior year in high school, with a mysterious ailment. I went to Africa to serve. I went to help. I didn't go to get ill. I had to sit out half of the cross-country season because they did not know if it was safe for me to train. After going around in circles for months, I decided that I didn't care anymore. I was going to run my senior year. I came back to the team so far behind, and I was a team captain at the time. How could I lead from behind? In the midst of not knowing what my health diagnosis would be I went back to what I knew, running. I even had a personal trainer from my church to work me out after races. He got me back in shape enough to return to the varsity squad and be a top finisher in our district.

After the season I told my team what I had gone through. Even then, I still didn't know what was wrong with me. For a couple years after that I would have episodes of the same pain and bleeding. I was nineteen in Korea when I was diagnosed with ovarian cysts and H. Pylori.

The torture of having something physically wrong with you that cannot be diagnosed or treated was enormous. I was just a teenager. I had to make up in my mind whether I would live in fear and restrict myself from enjoying life, or whether I would press forward and take the risks. My perception was, if they can't find it and prove that running will make it worse, then I'll take my chances. Running was my outlet and I couldn't give it away, ill or not.

ACKNOWLEDGE

Many times we struggle with the residual effects of pain because we are not willing to acknowledge that we were hurt by a person or situation. Sometimes pride doesn't want us to admit that someone had the ability to hurt us. For some reason we have the notion that if we don't admit we've been hurt, then we won't have to deal with the effects of being wounded in a situation. That notion is the furthest thing from the truth. Even if you do not admit it to the person who caused the pain, acknowledge and admit it to yourself. Be honest with your pain no matter how simple or small it may seem initially. When you avoid acknowledging something has occurred which pains you, you leave the door open for that wound to grow bacteria and implode. Avoidance may cause a simple wound to turn into an aggravated injury requiring painful interventions in order to heal.

We can be pained by situations that do not directly include or involve us. For example, children are usually affected when parents disagree, separate, divorce, etc. The parents' issues are with one another, however, the child is affected because the emotional state of the parents change towards one another, and many times it can also change towards the child. How many times have you seen children being withheld from one parent because the other parent was upset? Quality time and influencing children by how you live in front of them is greatly affected when a parent becomes absent.

Single parents where the other spouse chooses to be absent must admit they are hurt. Not just because the spouse doesn't want to be involved with them anymore, but because they have to watch their child/children endure the pain of rejection, loneliness, esteem changes, and endless questions or anger directed towards them. But because the child/children may feel it's their fault they've been abandoned. Parents who loves their child/children genuinely is always hurt by their child's/children's pain. Sometimes even when a child is suffering pain from consequences of their own actions a parent is still pained and may take partial responsibility. A child's wayward behaviors hurt the parents even if they have trained up that child the best way they know how.

When I was in middle school there was a teacher in the mentally gifted program who had a distaste concerning me. One day she said to me, "You'll never be anything." In the moment I did not feel pain, I felt anger. I would have never admitted to her that her statement was hurtful because I didn't feel like she deserved the satisfaction of knowing her words hurt me. I was about ten or eleven years old at the time and if that concept was embedded in my mind that young, imagine how many other pains I would fail to acknowledge in my life.

I have to admit that my self-esteem was hurt when I was teased about my looks. It wasn't always mean kids, but sometimes family members who would say things in a joking. I have to admit that failed relationships hurt me, even when I moved on to accomplished greater things in life and found new love. Truthfully speaking, I never enter into anything I plan to fail. I admitted the pain in being rejected and held back in ministry because I went to churches who did not believe in women preachers. This was painful because I felt my development was being stifled, while watching young males given opportunities. I have admitted that finding out people lied on me, talked negatively about me, scandalized my name, attempted to sabotage my family or relationships, or were prejudice towards me have inflicted some pain.

The longer you try to rationalize why things didn't hurt you that actually did, the longer you will hurt. The first pain may come from an external source, however, the greater pain begins when you deny your heart, mind, or soul the opportunity to tell its truth, "That hurt!" We too often have been taught that some things shouldn't hurt us. We internalize that and instead of those things actually not hurting us, we simply lie to ourselves and deny the hurt actually occurred.

Growing up we teach our children, "Sticks and stones may break my bones, but names will never hurt me." Names and words have been more painful than any physical injury I've experienced. What I have learned is to place a different level of value on the words depending upon the mouth it proceeds from. A stranger may say something to me and a close friend or relative says the same thing, but the words resonate on completely different levels.

The power of a word is connected to the perceived value of the vessel speaking it.

At one point any and every one could cause pain in my life, until I began to consider the source of the pain. Nevertheless, it is crucial for every person to acknowledge when their humanity has been offended, frustrated, or pained by another human, a situation, or the will of God. The very first phase of healing and productive energy comes from acknowledging the pain exists.

ACCEPT

Once acknowledgment occurs, the next step is accepting the pain for what it is. Many times when a person is experiencing some form of grief, one of the biggest barriers in grieving in a healthy manner is their inability, or unwillingness, to accept the loss.

Loss occurs in more situations than just the death of a loved one. It also occurs when something has ended that you were not ready to let go. This could be a relationship, romantic or platonic. A change either ends it, or causes it not to remain as close or vibrant as it once was. This could occur with an illness. Changes in health and strength occurring more rapidly than one is mentally prepared for can cause grief. For military personnel, moving to different assignments and having to start over every so often can cause grief and fear. Changes in financial status, declines in income, and no longer being able to afford the lifestyle you were accustomed to can cause grief.

We may not struggle with the fact pain has occurred, but sometimes we can get stuck on accepting it. We can try to avoid it, as if ignoring it will make it go away. We can try to explain why it couldn't be true. That is only lying to ourselves. We can argue about how it's not fair, but fairness isn't required for things to occur. We can insist it wasn't the end, but even if there is still hope of change, the pain has already occurred.

It is the past. You cannot change it now!

Time stands still for no one. With every second entering, another is exiting for all eternity. We are always living in the progressive moment; trying to enjoy the now, preparing for the next, but never able to reach backwards for change. Tormenting yourself with "what ifs" and "if I could've, would've...," "I should've..." delays your healing process.

Some pills are harder to swallow than others. The bottom line is we must accept what has occurred. By accepting it, we are not saying we like it, want it to be true, or approve of it happening. We are simply saying, it is real and I know it. Getting to a place of acceptance affords us an opportunity to pursue a change that is only possible to begin in the present. Once it begins it can evolve in the future for a completed process.

Oh what a relief it is when you learn to accept your truth. You free yourself to be honest with yourself. The worse form of deception is self-deception. When someone else deceives you, they know they are being dishonest with you. You are only deceived because to you it is truth. With self-deception you begin lying to yourself. That means you begin forcing yourself to believe something you are well aware is a lie. You force yourself to reject what your heart has experienced, and write over that memory with a forged signature of distortion.

Jeremiah references the heart as "deceitfully wicked, who can know it?"[1] Many times as preachers we teach this from the angle of needing a new heart from God, and not trusting your heart to keep you in God's will, and so forth. Yet the heart can be deceitful in how it processes pain, or refuses to process it. When the heart refuses to accept a pain, its memory sensations are smothered by a false reality, many times in self-defense and self-preservation efforts. The problem with this form of self-protection is that is does not make the pain go away. It covers the pain and hides it from view, only until the pain has an opportunity to reappear later in life. At the point of reappearance you have lost track of where the root of it originated, which only makes it harder to find the solution.

ASSESS (What's the depth and type of pain it is, whether preventable or destined, and whether you should/could be vulnerable to a reoccurring wound or not)

Every experience of pain does not require the same level of attention or treatment path. Learning how to assess the severity of the pain you are experiencing is necessary to identify what you must do to heal and become stronger from it. When my oldest son, Judah, is running around and falls and scrapes his knee he cries crocodile tears. I have to go pick him up, kiss his boo boo, and wipe his tears. I acknowledge that he is feeling pain, and teach him to accept that it has occurred. Afterwards I encourage him not to dwell on it long because that scratch will not hurt very long if he doesn't continue staring at it. However, when Judah fell on our bathroom floor and hit his head, my response was much different.

When Judah was about a year old, probably closer to eighteen months or so, I had given him a bath. He loved splashing water in his miniature tub so water was usually on the bathroom floor. I brought Judah into the bedroom with his towel on him. As I was getting his pajamas out of the drawer, he got up and ran back into the bathroom naked. Before I knew it all I heard was a loud splat, Judah holler, and then he became quiet. I ran into the bathroom and he was lying flat on his stomach with the side of his head on the floor. I picked him up immediately, turned him over, only to see his eyes rolling back. Despite being a registered nurse and having over ten years of medical experience and training, I panicked! My little baby was not responding to me! He was breathing and his heart was still beating, but he had a concussion.

I called my husband. He was out of town preparing to preach in a service, and I said frantically, "Judah fell and hit his head and I can't get him to wake up! You need to pray." He calmly told me to hang up and take Judah to the hospital. I didn't even know how to get to the children's hospital in Augusta. I called a member of the church who lived close who was a native to the city because in my mental state I could not drive. I remember putting his clothes on and trying to stimulate him and he just would not keep those eyes open. Even if he grimaced to my stimulation, he would quickly fall back asleep. Needless to say the seconds felt like hours, and the minutes felt like days in the process of getting out the house and to the hospital. He slept the whole way there, probably twenty minutes or so, and he did not wake up while I rushed from the parking lot into the hospital. He did not wake up until the admissions nurse did a rectal temperature. Then he cried and began reaching for me. Whew! Talking about being scared senseless.

We stayed in the children's emergency room for a couple hours. The physicians evaluated him and eventually he was back up playing and laughing. We were sent home and given instructions to watch for certain signs or symptoms that he was getting worse. I also looked for signals that he may have a headache and picked up medication to use as he healed. A Band-Aid and a kiss was not appropriate for this pain. He did get plenty of kisses and hugs throughout the situation although I knew it was different.

When it comes to pain, there are different degrees. It's like a burn. First-degree, second-degree, and third-degree burns are all burns, but they have different courses of action for treatment. The first-degree burn is like a sun-burn from staying out in the sun too long without any sunscreen. It is a very painful burn to touch. The skin is irritated and very sensitive. However, the treatment is fairly simple: cream, avoiding skin exposure, and allowing it to peel and heal. The second-degree burn is tender and may have blisters. It affects more than the top layer of skin and usually takes a couple to a few weeks to heal. The third-degree burn is not painful, although it is the worst of the three. It is not painful because the nerve endings and cells that transmit pain signals to the brain have been destroyed. This burn requires extensive treatment, and as the tissue heals, it goes from being painless to very painful.

An interesting fact about burns is that you can never have a third degree burn without second and first degree burns present. First degree burns are always present in every burn event. Which means there are multiple levels of healing and injury occurring at once. Understand that if you are experiencing a severe pain, the collateral damage includes every other level of pain beneath the worse level achieved. This means parts of your wound will heal at different rates. You cannot rush the severe pain to heal at the rate of the mild pain. Let each facet heal at its appropriate rate.

Some pains are like first degree burns, they are superficial. It doesn't take long to resolve if addressed quickly and the cause of the injury is avoided for a little while. A cooling period usually does the trick. After it heals the skin doesn't maintain a scar. Some pains don't leave a scar on your heart or mind. I like to call these casual offenses, usually committed by people who are either not close to you and may, or may not have been intentional. Or perhaps people who are close to you that were not intentionally offensive, who are immediately remorseful and apologetic.

The pain that begins to leave scars and alter the way we think in future situations I compare to second degree burns. It's not the worst pain, but it is painful enough to need more time to heal. The pain cuts beyond the surface and draws tears from your eyes. It affects the layer beneath what we are used to admitting or showing. This pain, if not treated, begins to change your view of a general population based on an individual's actions towards you. This pain requires active attention and time to get better.

The more severe pain is likened to third degree burns. With this burn you are advised not to try to treat it on your own, but to call 911 immediately. Unfortunately, because emotional and mental pain cannot be viewed physically with the eye, but is completely subjective, the person enduring the pain has to take an honest assessment of their own pain before anyone can know how to help.

Of course I recommend taking all pain to God in prayer. With the more severe pain, I also say, don't try to treat it by yourself. Reach out to a support group of friends, family, and community resources available to you. This pain is so deep that it rocks the very core of who you are. This pain alters your train of thought. This pain makes you think irrationally. This pain puts you in a mood that you cannot shake yourself out of by yourself. It doesn't have a healing timeline. It could take months, or even years to complete heal. And even after it heals, there is a permanent scar left at the site.

ASSIGN (A place for that pain to work in your favor)

When pain occurs, you must make a conscience decision concerning how that pain will work in your favor. Many times we just allow the pain to fester where it is and become bitter in that area. However, when you can begin assigning your pain a purpose it will not affect you in the same way it once did.

Think about when I was training for cross-country. I assigned the pain in my legs, back, and chest to my champion composition. I designated that soreness and intensity to my self-development files. Running those hills was making me physically stronger. Running those hills was making me mentally stronger. Running those hills was making me spiritually stronger, because of course I was praying for strength. The physical pain I endured in practice made the pain I felt in a race less intense. In practice I wasn't getting a break from the hills. I would run to the top, jog to the bottom, and run right back to the top. Generally in races the hills were more spaced out. So in a race I would tell myself, just make it to the top because there's a break from the uphill inclines after this. And generally speaking, there was usually a nice downhill after the uphill I could fly down and regroup on.

You see because I was such a light weight, if the downhill was steep enough, all I had to do was make sure my feet didn't get stuck and gravity would practically take me down the hill. I remember running at the Belmont Plateau in Philadelphia. In the wooded area of the course there was a hill called "parachute" that was followed by a steep downhill called "suicide." Now going up Parachute is where many people started walking because by that point you had already run over a mile. Here no one could see you except the few people assigned to ensure no one was cheating or injured. Otherwise, your coach wasn't there to yell at you. Your family couldn't see you walking. Your teammates wouldn't know if you were walking unless they were coming up from behind you. I remember running up the steep hill and being amazed that some people started walking at the top of the hill or stood still to take a breath. I kept moving, because although my legs were heavy and sometimes felt like lead, I knew that "suicide" was coming and all I had to do was go with it. That was the best part of the race! Even though I wasn't naturally a sprinter, but going down that hill I was my fastest! In order for me to have the physical and mental stamina to make it to the top of the hill without stopping, I had to assign my pain a purpose. I had no idea I would get paid to run in college, but that pain I assigned a purpose at the age of fourteen would bring me dividends in my twenties and even throughout my military career for physical fitness requirements.

When I began to inventory the unassigned pains in my life, I saw that every pain I did not give an assignment was able to run its own agenda in my life. Usually its agenda was to weaken me, produce fear, doubt, hatred, anger, malice, suspicion, etc. in my heart and mind. I got to a point where I did not want to give people or situations that much power over me. This was, in fact, my life to live and not anyone else's puppet show to control.

If you do not assign your pain to a positive designated area in your life, you run the risk of simply being infected and not just affected by it.

Being affected by pain speaks to the response you have to the cause of that pain. If I am cut with a knife while cooking, the effects of that would be a breaking of my skin, possible bleeding, and pain. Those effects will not last very long. However, if I am bit by a cat and do not properly treat it, an infection could rapidly set in. This infection would cause my hand to swell and could require urgent surgery with antibiotic treatment. Waiting too long to treat this infection could render permanent tissue damage to their hand.

Both injuries may have very small puncture sites on the hand. However, the results of these wounds could end very differently. Your pain may appear too small for concern. But be aware that even the smallest punctures left unattended can produce the greatest complications.

When I burned my hand on an iron, I assigned it to my "lessons learned" file. In doing so, in the future I was more aware of the heat and how I handled an iron. I did not get mad at the iron for burning me, or resolve to never iron my clothes again because I had been burned by an iron. I realized that I was burned because of how I mishandled the iron, and learned not to be so nonchalant with objects that could burn me. I'm saying this to remind you that some things, people, and situations may have burned you, but it's not for you to say "I'll never deal with that situation again," or for you to avoid that person or group of people for the rest of your life. Sometimes it's just for you to file it in your "lessons learned" file and choose to handle it with better care and attention in the future.

As you process the pain don't forget to acknowledge that an undesired harm has occurred. Accept that it has happened and cannot be undone. Assess it to discover how simple or serious its affects are. Finally, assign it a place to produce a positive return in your life.

Malcolm X said "There is no better than adversity. Every defeat, every heartbreak, every loss, contains its own seed, its own lesson on how to improve your performance next time." There is no need to run from opposition, use it to your advantage!

3

Beginning the Healing

Believe it or not, we are in control of when our healing begins. Too often we choose to wallow in the pain of injuries to our hearts and minds. I used to struggle with beginning to move forward and heal because I was waiting on people to apologize to me, or feel remorseful for their actions towards me, or for them to change. That is so far from reality!

*Waiting on others to encourage you, inspire you, or free
you to begin healing is like waiting for a public
transportation bus to pick you up in between bus stops.*

It's possible that it could happen, but less likely
than you just going to a bus stop and waiting. When you
are finished feeling sorry for yourself, being angry over the
situation, looking for sympathy or offering yourself pity
parties, then you are ready to begin the healing process. Let
me warn you, some healing is just as painful as the injury
itself.

In the previous chapter we learned how to assess our
pain. We compared the degrees of injury to burn degrees.
First and second degree burns begin very painful and
gradually hurt less and less. However, third degree burns
start off with no pain simply because the nerve endings are
burned so the person cannot feel the pain.

The treatment of third degree burns involves
removing all the charred skin (debridement), that which is
completely destroyed tissue. Removing all the damaged
tissue down to what's healthy is crucial. These patients are
taken to a room where they are literally scrubbed down to
the healthy skin. I spoke with an intensive care nurse,
James Ryals, who had experience with burn care. He said,
"If you've never cried with a patient before, you will cry
then." These patients are in so much pain trying to get
healed that it hurts everyone watching. They definitely
need pain medication before and after the procedure.
Depending on how much body surface is covered the
patient could be sedated during treatment to prevent them

from going into shock from the level of pain experienced in debriding.

DEBRIDEMENT

Uncover and remove the damaged and infected feelings from your memory. You have to scrape off the layers of dead weight that's covering the healthy you. The healthy skin will not grow over the damaged skin. New skin cells grow from beneath the current level of skin, and the outer level sheds to make way for it. It's the same with emotions. Healthy emotions and mindsets, do not grow on top of damaged areas.

So many times we have grown accustomed to sweeping things under the rug. Instead of dealing with our pain, we would rather numb it by distracting ourselves with other activities. Some people distract themselves with work. The more they hurt, the longer their hours at work get. They drown themselves in project after project, keeping their mind preoccupied with business so they can ignore the inner voice crying out for help. Some people distract themselves with family. They become the problem solver and hero for their family and friends. This way they don't have to face their own wounded souls. Some people distract themselves with religion. They use religion to make them feel better, receiving temporary boosts to make it through the hard times. Some people distract themselves with substances: smoking, drinking, pills, shooting up. We all have our "drug" of choice. We all have something we use to escape the pressures of our reality. Some people use exercise, other people eat, shop, or sleep.

Escaping is no way to heal. While you can escape from others, you can never escape from yourself.

Wherever you try to hide, you will always find yourself. Wherever you try to run away to, you will be followed by your wounded self. Whatever world you try to create to keep others from knowing your hurting state, you will be there to declare that fantasy a lie. Your mind, body, and soul can never be divided until you die. As long as there's breath in your body, you will not escape your hurting self.

You may be able to ignore your pain for a season. You may be able to turn the volume down on that voice temporarily. However, one thing I can tell you for a fact is that voice will speak again. After while it will come through in your thought process, subconscious actions, and your character.

One of the reasons debridement is essential for burn victims is they have a very high risk of infection. Because skin is the body's first line of defense against infection, with a damaged barrier all organisms that are normally kept out of the body have access in. Therefore, special precautions are made to protect the person by keeping other people at a distance, and making those who come close wear protective barriers.

How many times have we seen infections occur mentally and emotionally? Signs of infection are elevated temperature, elevated heart rate, foul odor, and drainage from the physical site. Signs of emotional infection are bitterness, frustration, agitation, hatred, malice, resentment, easily provoked to wrath, and being in prolonged states of emotions meant to be temporary. Signs of mental infection are depression, mental breakdowns, confusion, uneasiness, restlessness, and inability to focus, concentrate, or be productive.

Does your attitude stink? Does your presence give off negative auras to others? Do people avoid you? Are your relationships on the verge of breaking up? Have you become disconnected from people or things you should be attached to? Have your feelings that were once hot, waxed cold? Are you walking around numb in your life?

While you're in debridement it's imperative to keep negative people at a distance. People who are doubtful, antagonistic, sarcastic, or bitter will only add to the infection. Their words are like bacteria in an incubator. They sink into your heart and mind, which are the incubators of your life, and reproduce. The best way to stop the infection is an antibiotic. Something used to prevent the bacteria from replicating.

We cannot control what events have already caused us to be infected. The past is behind us. There's no magical potion or time machine to take us backwards. Nothing that's been done can be altered. Only what is in the present moment can we affect. So how do we keep negative thoughts from replicating?

DESENSITIZE

Learn your trigger points, what reminds you of the event, or brings back the bad feelings, and disassociate those things if possible. The more you rehearse the event in your mind, the deeper your wound becomes. Every time you choose to relive the event in your mind, notice how you dig deeper and deeper for more painful details. This is especially true when you're sharing the details of the event with people who wish to fan the flames, instead of extinguishing them.

Desensitizing can occur through different methods. While I would love to completely avoid the memory of certain events in my life, I have found it nearly impossible! So if I am left with constant reminders, then my emotional response to those triggers has to change.

One reason we remain as sensitive as we are to situations is the way we rehearse them in our mind. Every time we think about it, we view ourselves as the victim. We usually label the offender as the villain, and make ourselves completely innocent and helpless. Victimizing ourselves only makes us angrier that someone did something TO US. Think about what you tell yourself. "How could they do that to me?" "How could they treat me this way?" "After all I've done for them, why would they hurt me like this?" "How did I deserve that?" "What did I do to provoke this? I've never done anything to hurt them this way."

Instead of torturing yourself with the helpless approach, your perception has to change. For veterans with post-traumatic stress disorder, one recommendation is to make the soldier revisit the event repeatedly until they can think about it without feeling the overwhelming negative emotions. It is helpful when revisiting painful memories to search for the positive angles that do exist.

Instead of looking at the betrayal as an insult to your love, loyalty, and trust in a person, see it as a means of testing how pure your love is. In today's society we use the term "I love you" so loosely. Many people who say it, have no idea what it really means to have true love for another person. Love is an action word that gives patience, kindness, forgiveness, compassion, and acceptance to someone freely, without stipulations, or the need to be paid back by equal behavior or efforts from the other person.

Pure love is not predicated on what the other person does or doesn't do. Love is simply a gift you choose to give to someone else. Love is in its purest form when you choose to give it to someone who does not appear to deserve it.

So when people close to me have done things to hurt me, even severely, I evaluate my love's purity in the situation. I make a conscious decision to focus on what I can control, change, and consider my growth from the situation. What have I learned that I wouldn't have if this never occurred? What knowledge or wisdom wouldn't have been added to my life because of this crossroad? How has my character improved by encountering someone else's lack of character? How did they drive me to do better in how I treat others?

I look back to see what the warning signs were that I was at risk of being hurting by this person? Why did I ignore those signs? What can I do differently next time I observe similar warning signs in other relationships? Am I going to allow this to tear me down? Am I going to allow this to shatter my world? Haven't I made it through other difficult times? Why can't I also make it through this one?

I remember in grade school I had my first "boyfriend." Man, he was just the cutest, smartest, most amazing boy in the world to me. He was my first love. He was my first kiss. He was the first guy I danced with. I just knew we were inseparable. Inevitably we broke up and wow, that thing hurt so much. At that time it was the worse pain I had ever experienced in romance. I couldn't believe it. Puppy love was crushed.

Needless to say, we both moved on. Dated other people and progressed down different life paths. When I think about the break up now, I am not devastated at all. I've had so many other life experiences that I am not sensitive to that breakup anymore. Many of you reading likely remember your first love, and majority of you probably didn't make it. However, your next love may have gotten stronger and stronger. The more you learned what love meant, the more you realized what you were so crushed over wasn't as heartbreaking as you thought it was. Although it may seem harsh to say, some of our biggest heartbreaks were necessary to give room for the genuine love experiences to enter our lives.

When I reflect on some of my horrific experiences these two main things have helped desensitize me to my initial feelings, time and perspective. Some hurt less in the process of time. Other things hurt less when my mindset changed towards the situation.

In late 2004, I lost two grandparents, only two months apart. My maternal grandfather, Thornton H. Goff Jr., died in October after battling renal cancer. I won't forget the phone call I got from my god-brother David, who was back in Philadelphia. I was a young soldier stationed in Columbus, GA. I hadn't been home since the December prior and at that time my grandfather appeared normal. However, since that time he'd lost so much weight I didn't even recognize him in recent pictures. Somehow he convinced my family not to tell me and my brother Iric, who was also away in the military. My grandfather didn't want to worry us. No one ever told us he was ill with cancer. David called me and said very calmly, "Cece, I just couldn't keep this from you anymore. It's just not right. You need to come home, Pop-pop isn't doing well." I remember being very confused. How could he be gradually getting sicker and no one took the time to tell us he was even sick? I could've made plans to come home on leave. Why didn't he tell me when we spoke on the phone?

I asked David, "What exactly is going on?" At that time all he could say was, he's in the hospital and it's not looking good. "Get here as soon as possible." I hung up with him and contacted my first line supervisor to find out what I needed to do to get home to Philadelphia. We got the Red Cross message and I submitted my paperwork.

While I was waiting on the commander to sign my emergency leave, I got another phone call saying "I'm sorry. He's gone."

Talk about a blow to the chest! How could all of this have transpired in a matter of hours? I just found out he had cancer, and I was preparing to get there to see him. Before I could even get my paperwork signed he was dead. I didn't even get to talk to him. I didn't get to say goodbye. My first emotion towards him and my family was anger. I couldn't believe they would keep something this important from my brother and me.

I was close to my grandfather. He was my pastor. He coached me before my preaching engagements and prayed with me. Although he couldn't license me when I accepted my call to the ministry, he supported me. Thankfully, he had the opportunity to hear me preach in a youth revival I coordinated at his church December of 2013. I still have the VHS where he spoke afterwards. He was so proud of me. Our birthdays were seven days apart. He'd just celebrated his pastoral anniversary in September and to my knowledge, he was doing well.

This was a hard one to get over. I was angry because I felt like they denied me an opportunity to grieve in the process with them. When I arrived home to Philadelphia, I was so mad I didn't even go to my see that side of my family until the following day when my brother arrived. I went to my dad's house and stayed in the room by myself. It took time for me to get over that. I had to forgive my grandfather for making them swear and promise they wouldn't tell me. I had to forgive my mother, aunts, cousins, etc. for not breaking their promise to him to tell me anyway.

It took years for me to get over that. In time I understood that he was suffering and very anxious about his health. Reading some of his personal writings in those last months helped me see how desperate he was for God to heal him. He was begging God to heal him so he could do His will. But God's will was for him to complete his work. My grandfather hated to see everyone worrying about him. He was the leader. He was the pastor. He was the father. He was the husband. He was the man. He wanted to be strong for us, all the while he was weaker than he'd ever been. The least my family members thought they could do was honor his wishes. They didn't expect for him to die. If they knew he was that close to death they would've called me sooner. Nobody knew it was the end.

I worked through the pain that week by writing my grandfather a song. The song is entitled "Don't Cry." I sang the song every day, over and over at the church. I played the piano and Iric played the drums. We both sang it while looking at the pulpit chair covered in black drapes. We sang it until we could get through it without crying. At the funeral, we sang our tribute and everyone else cried but us. I didn't know it then but what I was doing I see now I was desensitizing in order to be productive at his home-going service. When I returned to Georgia, I had some friends help me record the song and I gave my family members copies of it that Christmas when I returned to Philly.

On my way home for Christmas I picked up my paternal grandmother, Nana, from South Carolina. She stayed at my dad's house that week and rode back home with me and my close friend Michelle. Michelle and I were preparing for a New Year's Eve service in North Carolina. We were on program to mime and we were excited to get there and see our friends. We dropped my grandmother home and hastened along. She wanted us to stay and eat, but after a twelve hour ride with a few more hours to go, we just wanted to leave.

Finally, we arrived Fayetteville and while relaxing with some friends my dad called me. In his calm voice he told me, "Your nana was in a car accident." I asked was she okay; what hospital is she at? I was going to go back and see her the next morning. He said, "She's not in the hospital." I was thinking, "Oh good. She wasn't hurt too bad, she's already back home." That was not the case. She wasn't in the hospital because she died at the scene.

Talk about a phone dropping moment. I just left her! She was fine. She was happy. She was alive. She had just comforted my other grandmother on how to live as a widow. She'd been doing it for four years at that point, and she encouraged my grandmother, Diana, on how to heal and get through the hard days, weeks, months, and years to come. Lugenia McClurkin, my nana, was just as sweet as she could be.

How could God hit me that hard again...SO SOON? Didn't He remember how he took my grandfather only two months prior? How much did He think I could take? How rude of Him to not let me grieve good from the first loss, and here I am losing another grandparent.

This time I felt guilty for leaving her. Maybe if I had stayed longer she wouldn't have been driving that day. I could've taken her where she needed to go. We never discovered what caused the accident, but if I was with her I could've been there to help her. And there I was stuck! Stuck between my aching heart and still praising God in Watch Night service. While this is a night when the preacher always says, "Thank God you made it into another year!" How could I thank God and my grandmother had just died in a tragic accident?

The only thing that soothed my pain in this situation was knowing the last week of her life was full of joy and she was surrounded by family. She didn't suffer long. She was just with me and she knew I love her very much.

These two deaths were so different in how they unfolded, however, they both hurt severely. Only through the process of time has the sting of death burned less. When remembering the scenarios surrounding their deaths, I have to look through different eyes than I did at the time. That's the only way I could make it through the grieving process. I had to learn it is okay not to stay depressed. I had to learn it didn't mean I loved them any less if I didn't constantly look at their pictures. They often come to my mind, and I still have both obituaries, but I don't talk about it too often.

Death is something none of us can control. It never seems fair. Life never seems long enough. The situation never seems to come at the right time. Even though we all know life is only a vapor, we expect it to be everlasting. Death brings about a hurtful experience none of us can avoid. Yet over time, the pain slowly gets more and more bearable. Separation by death is one of the few permanent changes in life that occur. Many other hurtful situations we face have the potential of being changed. Relationships with friends that hurt us can be mended if we're willing. Relationships with family that offends us, can be mended if we're willing.

Never make permanent decisions based on temporary situations or emotions.

DEVELOPMENT

Build yourself up with healthy interests and ideas, and relationships or experiences. I was watching Christian television one day when I saw a woman testifying about how she had lost both her children in a tornado, but is now an even more adamant grief counselor/minister for her church. As I watched her interview I couldn't help but think to myself, I don't think I could do that so soon after losing my boys. The love a mother has for her children is one of the strongest bonds in the world. How could she lose so much and come out so strong?

Life is choice driven. You either actively choose to take actions to improve your life, or passively choose to allow events to degrade the quality of life you have.

This woman chose to turn her tragedy into her strongest tool to heal herself by helping others. She knows she can't change the fact she lost both her children, but she can change how grieving people survive after losing their loved ones. There is no doubt in my mind her heart is still bruised and tender. I have no doubt she doesn't have days where she just cries it out. I'm certain she has some dreadful nights. But, somehow she has chosen to not be broken to the point of being crippled, but broken to a place of unlimited compassion and openness.

When I sat down to write this book I was at a crossroad. Either I would be overcome by emotions of disappointment, sorrow, grief, frustration, anger, etc. or I'd use my personal pain to teach myself lessons I could share with others. I chose the latter because it was the best way to navigate through the sea of emotions on my heart and thoughts on my mind.

There is a power activated within when we choose to grow from struggles and not succumb to the alternative.

Although in math, two negatives multiplied together equals a positive; in life negative with negative leaves negative. You must outnumber your negativity with positivity. One of the ways to achieve this is through personal development.

FORTIFICATION

If we are honest with ourselves, a portion of the hurt we endure in this life is due to bad decisions we have made.

We allowed people to get too close, too soon, and they caused too much damage. Sometimes, due to impatience and desperation, we became clingy in our vulnerable states and attached ourselves to people who never intended us any good. We liked their personality. We liked their looks. We may have liked their influence or position. We found things attractive about them and engaged in friendships or relationships, all the while ignoring the bigger flaws that were so apparent. Why do we settle? Many times it's because of how we view ourselves.

Not having a clear understanding of who you are, and what you're worth will always leave you vulnerable to degrading relationships.

It's kind of like trying to sell your car back to a dealership. I had a very nice car. It turned heads everywhere I went. It set me apart in some people's mindset. Just the name Jaguar, was enough to have people respect me a little more. To them it meant I had money. I had prestige. I was financially established. Because I had purchased the car used, the prior owner had done some things to it that I was paying for. After a while I decided to go back and get the car I really wanted. I sought to find it with no prior accidents, as new as I could without paying the new car price. I didn't need two cars, so I wanted to sell or trade in my Jaguar.

I went to a couple local dealerships and they began offering me some really low numbers. If I was uninformed of my car's worth I would've been gullible and lost thousands of dollars. I knew good and well that the same dealer who offered me a low price would turn around and mark it up at least five to seven thousand dollars more for the next buyer. I knew the condition and quality of my car, and I refused to settle. I held on to it a little longer and ended up selling it for more than I was aiming for. Someone else valued it more than the other dealerships had, and even more than I was beginning to think it was worth.

I learned a valuable lesson in that process. I found I must to determine the value of my possessions, or else others will quickly try to devalue them so they could make a bigger profit. Likewise, I also know this truth, you have to determine the value of yourself and display that to others, or else others will come and treat your china like disposable plates.

If you don't think enough to fortify yourself, you are advertising your lack of self-worth.

Fortifying yourself means to safeguard your access points, and repair the breaches in your walls. In the old days places were fortified by their walls that surrounded the cities. If the walls were poorly built, falling down, had holes and missing pieces, the enemy could easily access the city from any angle and raid the place. The purpose of the wall and gate was to make people enter and exit at the designated place.

Search yourself and find out where you are most vulnerable. Evaluate why you are vulnerable there. Then work towards strengthening that access point. Everyone is not meant to be in your inner circle. Some people must stay on the outer realm because they cannot handle access to your heart. I learned to permit people space to earn their way into my secret place. I could not give a free admission pass to the seat of my emotions.

FOCUS

Another important part of development is being able to focus. Where is your focus? What is it on? How important is the object of your focus? In five years will it still be important? Are you accomplishing your goals? Or are you good at starting and never finishing anything? What has your attention gripped?

It took me many years to figure out how to take time to focus on ME. I was always focused on how I could help others. I wanted to be the hero and save the world from their problems. I wanted to be the one to help everyone else achieve their goals and dreams. I wanted to be the shoulders that everyone stood on to get up. I was never a crab in the bucket, but always a step stool.

That mindset has its place. However, what I discovered was that I was helping others' dreams come true and my own dreams were dying. I was solving others' problems and my problems were piling up. I was building up others and I was being torn down. The truth is I am more effective as a helper when I first learn to help myself. If I settled myself and focused on developing my skills and mindset, then my ability to improve those around me would reach further.

To focus means you are concentrating on an objective with full enthusiasm and not easily distracted by other things. Focus requires discipline. It means you must maintain the fact that your objective is more important than the various distractions coming your way. You must get so focused on improving yourself, that at times your vision becomes tunneled.

Tunneled vision is often times considered negative. When it's time to begin healing from pain tunneling your vision is one of your best companions. Focus is the greatest distraction from wallowing in pain. It causes you to move past situations quicker because you are too busy to sulk. Focus puts a fire under you to achieve a goal. It clears up your vision for what is truly important and significant. Focus shifts your life by shifting your eyes and interests.

EDUCATE

Development is never as powerful as it should be without proper information and wisdom. As I watch my oldest son grow through his toddler years, I realize he has no idea how much stronger he's become in the last couple of years. I watch him interact with his infant brother and I'm constantly telling him: don't press there, don't lean on him, don't lay on him, be careful. He doesn't understand that how he leans on me to get up, he can't do to his brother. He does know that he's getting bigger. He can tell he's getting taller. He understands he's able to do things he wasn't able to do months ago. He's developing simply because he's eating and living.

When Judah was just an infant I was constantly at the doctor's office so they could monitor his height and weight because they declared he was underweight and under height for his age. He was beneath the standard growth curve and the healthcare providers were getting adamant about what I was or wasn't feeding him. Between the age of one and two we even had a consultation with a nutritionist. We found out that he wasn't getting as much food per day as he should. We weren't depriving him of food, his appetite just wasn't there. He got so used to drinking milk that he wanted to fill up on milk bottles more than eating solid foods.

Milk is supposed to do a body good. I didn't see much wrong with him drinking so much milk. At least it wasn't juice and junk. He'd lived off of milk for a while and he was just a short little boy, much like his parents, and he had a pot belly like most toddlers. He didn't look malnourished. Yet through education I found out more ways to ensure he took in more food groups each day. I also discovered, he learned his eating habits from staying with his dad every day while I was at work. My husband drinks fluids all day and only eats one good meal a day and maybe a snack. Of course Judah doesn't eat much! He doesn't see much food. We had to learn to sit him down at his table without distractions to ensure that he ate.

My other son, Zion, is the complete opposite. He is growing faster than expected and is developing because his parents are more educated through book knowledge and experience. I'm sure he will probably walk sooner than

Judah did and be engaged and encouraged to do things sooner because I know he is capable of it.

If you are going to ever heal and begin transforming pain into power, you must learn from the lessons presented to you in this life. If you continue to face the same situations over and over, it may be that you haven't passed the test. Are you paying attention to the class you're in? You will only graduate from here by passing the test. Life's tests aren't like quick tests in school that you can memorize answers long enough to pass the test, and then forget it all right after you pass. Life has a way of doing a "check on learning" when you least expect it.

Where you've failed repeatedly seek knowledge and wisdom in that area so you can avoid failing again. After failing in an area of life multiple times with multiple people, then it's time to look inward and learn what you're doing wrong. What do I need to change in order to win? What do I need to strengthen in order to win? Instead of being frustrated and quitting, get frustrated enough to improve yourself.

You are in control of your healing process. How bad do you want to stop hurting? How much responsibility are you willing to take in your own healing? How much do you love yourself?

"A journey of a thousand miles begins with a single step" (Chinese Proverb). The beginning of your healing is waiting on you to take the first step. Why not start the journey today?

LaChish Latimer

4

Forgiveness

I would always hear people say "Forgiveness isn't for the other person, it's for you." I honestly did NOT believe that one bit. I used to feel people didn't deserve forgiveness unless they apologized sincerely for the offense they caused. Depending on how serious the offense was, even after an apology I was still reluctant to forgive; especially if I thought they should've known better than to have ever done that. Even when I finally did forgive, I had the hardest time moving forward because I could not forget it.

Today my perspective has changed drastically. Although I cannot say I've mastered this yet, I have certainly come a mighty long way. In this chapter I plan to present the information like an attorney to a jury, and will allow you to draw your own conclusion at the end. Some steps may not be applicable to every pain you will experience, but principles should work regardless of the details.

Okay, let's get into it: To forgive or not to forgive…that is the question.

When I look back over the course of my life, certain situations have rocked the core of my being. Those things I can quickly recall to my mind, however, other offenses I've practically forgotten. Offenses that caused feelings of betrayal, abandonment, endangerment, or perceived malice towards me by an enemy have been the hardest things for me to forgive. What has been even harder are those same offenses done by someone I considered a friend, brother, or sister.

WHY CONSIDER FORGIVENESS?

Maya Angelou said something that resonated with me on an interview. She said, "I am a human being; nothing human can be alien to me." What she was saying was to never look at any act committed by another human as something impossible for you to commit as well. I was so guilty of this! I could look at the news and see things that people had done, or watch a television show, or experience a situation and I would be so agitated at the perpetrator because I just could not see myself ever doing anything like they'd done.

I watched people abuse kids, and hit them too hard, or snap on a child. Watching that would make me want to strangle that person because it was just so cruel to me, and unfair because the child is so defenseless. Then God showed me how I was capable of snapping myself. Although I have never abused either of my children I remember one night when I was just extremely exhausted caring for my son Zion when he was a newborn. I was home alone with my three year old and the baby. Zion literally cried for three hours unless I got up and walked around with him. By 3 a.m. I was so agitated that he was inconsolable. I tried feeding him. I gave him gas medicine. I burped him. I changed him. I sang to him. I did all the things I knew to soothe him, but could not. Judah was asleep. I'm not sure how he stayed asleep with all that noise. I remember looking at Zion face to face and saying "Please stop crying!" By this time, I was ready to cry myself! At that moment I thought about how frustrated I was getting and I believe Zion could also sense that. I also thought about how as a nurse I've seen babies come into the emergency room who were shaken vigorously. When the perpetrator is interviewed, they usually say, the baby wouldn't shut up and they got frustrated and before they knew it, had shaken the baby till they were quiet.

Whoa! Here I am very frustrated, and extremely tired. I want my baby to be quiet and he won't stop crying. I'm human enough to also make a really bad decision in the heat of the moment. However, what kept me from choosing that option was my awareness of my frustration, and my intelligence to know that sometimes infants are colicky but it will pass. So I began to cater to Zion in whatever way he found soothing. Then I learned he liked to look at the lights on the television. So I stood by the television until he calmed himself down, then gradually moved back to my bed, and he fell asleep for a few hours. I was so happy I didn't snap or make a poor decision because that was my precious baby. His only form of communication was crying at that time.

You may not relate to that, but then I also experienced a car accident. I've been in a few, most of them I was not at fault. But there was one time I was driving at night to visit a friend who lived almost four hours away. I remember how excited I was because my friend had been deployed and was home now. I couldn't wait to get there and celebrate the fact they made it back safely and without any major injuries. I was only ten minutes from my destination and I was approaching a stop light. The light had already turned green, however, the cars that were at the light while it was red had not pulled off yet. Before I knew it I was slamming on my brakes, and BOOM! I hit the back of a big SUV in my 2004 Honda CRV. My air bag did not deploy. I got out of my car and walked to the driver's window of the car I just hit. The driver was okay, very agitated with me of course, but physically okay. Unfortunately, there was a little girl in the back seat, between ten to thirteen years olds, and she was hysterical! She was screaming and crying and very upset. I asked her if she was physically hurt. During this time I was an emergency medical technician, so I was concerned with her assessment. When we pulled our cars over to the side of the road, we discovered she was not physically harmed, but emotionally shaken up. Whew! This could've been so much worse.

Just that quick, because of my lack of judgment in a critical moment I could have hurt someone's child. I've never been a drinker, so would never have a DUI (driving under the influence) experience. Even still I have driven many times while tired. When I would hear of tragic car accidents and that the driver who caused the accident was drunk or something, it would disgust me. Then I thought about how although I don't choose to drink and drive, I have driven and placed myself and others at risk. Of course in my logic, I never intentionally set out to hurt anyone, but it's rare that others do either.

It got to a point where everything I was disgusted at I would come face to face with so that I could see how I too was at risk of committing the same offenses. Jesus speaks of a woman who loves much because she's been forgiven much. He says that she loves greater because she realizes that she's been forgiven for a great deal of offenses herself. However, those who have been forgiven very little, also tend to love very little as well [2]. This is where I am in my heart. God has truly forgiven me from a slew of secret sins in my heart, mind, and even in deeds. When I begin thinking about how offensive I've been to my God, who has always been faithful to me even when I didn't like Him, wouldn't talk to Him, wouldn't thank Him or praise Him or acknowledge Him, it humbles me.

I think about the people I've hurt unintentionally and in my ignorance and am humbled by the grace of God. I look at how I used to be so quick tempered and fighting and cursing people out. I was rude and not afraid of anybody. I'm still not afraid of people. I fought girls, boys, men, and women. Here I am five foot tall, less than one hundred pounds, and full of hostility. I try not to allow myself to get pushed to that point anymore, but sometimes I battle with wanting to "go off" simply because I feel people try to take advantage of my kindness or patience. What keeps me from being foolish is the debt I owe to God for the many offenses I've been forgiven. God has saved more people than may be aware by helping me with self-control. That's a good place to smile.

HOW IS IT FOR ME?

There is a principle that says that if you don't forgive others, you will not be forgiven by God[3]. I tell people often, you can tell which parts of your Faith's doctrine you really believe by which part you live by and apply. I obviously didn't believe this text was true. I couldn't have believed it because I refused to do it. Even after reading it and studying it I would not do it. I figured God would have to forgive me because the only thing that's unforgiveable is blasphemy. Since I wasn't blasphemous I was fine. I figured I was good with God because of all the other things I was doing according to the scriptures. Surely that would balance out with not forgiving people who intentionally caused me harm. Obviously, God was mad at these people too!

One day the light bulb came on and wow, what an epiphany! It really wasn't that complicated or deep. God simply wants His children to walk in His likeness. For those who advertise that we are submitted to God, we are charged with being advertisements for Him. We become walking billboards that are often watched, observed, and critiqued to see what difference our God really makes in our lives. People who do not believe, and many times people who do, are watching to see if inviting God into your heart has caused you to respond and react to life's challenges any different from others who do not profess to be in relationship with a higher power.

Forgiveness is not a natural ability, it is a supernatural gift shared with humanity.

When you forgive, you begin to operate in an elevated sense of purpose and ability. Human nature is all about self-preservation, self-fulfillment, and self-indulgence.

To forgive is to sacrifice of yourself for another person who is least qualified of receiving any gifts from you at that time.

Yes, forgiveness is a gift you give to a person who has caused you pain, distress, and grievances. Forgiveness is an act of love, kindness, and grace shown upon a person in need of mercy. Forgiveness has nothing to do with the offense committed. It also does not mean you approve or support any of the actions this person commits. It is not an endorsement for others to continue hurting you either. It is not a sign of weakness, or being gullible. Although you may feel like a fool, you are actually operating in wisdom when you forgive.

Even for those who don't believe in Jesus Christ, the golden rule all humanity can relate to. "Treat others as you want to be treated." When you reflect on your own ability as a human, living in the flesh, with all your frailties to become an offense to someone else, you too would desire mercy. When life begins to treat you unfairly, and your judgment is cloudy, and your actions are not always within your normal character, you will want mercy. When fear, hurt, doubt, frustration, anger, confusion, or ignorance become an overwhelming influence and you make poor decisions, you will desire mercy. And if you are ever temporarily out of your normal frame of mind and make irrational decisions, when you come back to yourself, you will desire forgiveness.

Forgiveness gives God an opportunity to avenge you.

God declares, "Vengeance is mine saith the Lord, I will repay"[4]. Many times I really did not want to give God His chance to avenge me because it seemed like He took too long to do it. Sometimes I wanted the satisfaction of getting even myself. What was actually happening in my heart was I wanted the other person to hurt just as much, if not more than I was hurting. I asserted myself as the offender after being offended. But the way God set things up for me was simply to shield me from placing myself in the need of forgiveness for causing someone else pain.

God asks us to let Him take vengeance to keep us innocent. When you take time to really think about the way God orchestrates things, He tries to keep you out of trouble.

This principle is true, you will reap what you sow. Not only does forgiving others cause you to receive the forgiveness of others, but it prevents you from sowing negative seeds that you will reap in the form of a harvest. Think about how small a seed is. Seeds come in all different shapes and sizes. One thing is guaranteed from every seed, it will always produce something greater in size and capacity. Although you may feel justified in retaliating, or defending yourself, you are simply sowing seeds to reap an even worse harvest. The intentions or reasons for planting the seed can't change the law of the principle, you HAVE TO reap what you sow.

True justice comes from a greater source than you.

Although you feel you are able to compensate your pain on your own, God has a greater reach than you ever will. Also, justice is only true when it is carried out by someone who is not emotionally driven by the offense. God loves us dearly, however, He does not deal with people permanently based on temporary distaste or discontentment with them. God is so just that He can chastise you in one moment and comfort you in the next. God is not out to break us in a destructive manner, but always constructive.

When we allow Him to distribute vengeance, His aim is to make the offender better. Our intentions are rarely considerate of their potential or purpose, or damage which motivated their offensive behavior in the first place.

With our plans in place we are more likely to potentiate the cycle of inducing pain than we are to alleviate or eradicate the cycle. I was raised to think, if you hit me I must hit you back. I didn't want to be bullied. I didn't want to be perceived as weak. I didn't want to become a target for others to prey on. The older and more mature I become, the more I realize the power of being an example. I've never been one to follow blindly. Yet when it came to unforgiveness and revenge, I didn't realize I was simply following the lead of the person who offended me. God forbid! Who wants to be like the person who has angered or pained them? Logically thinking, no one! Reality is our thinking isn't logical when we are pained. The pain distracts us and can consume us if we are not careful.

HOW DO I REALLY FORGIVE?

Forgiveness is very difficult, and maybe even impossible when you are constantly replaying the incident in your mind. Every time you think about it, and dwell on it, you become sensitive to the pain all over again. You give life to the past, and overshadow the present with negative influences that would otherwise be gone.

Some would suggest that forgiveness is a one-time event, however, forgiveness is needed every time you relive the experience in your heart and mind.

Peter asked Jesus, how many times should we forgive a person for offending us? Seven times? Jesus replied seventy times seven[5]. When I think of human nature, I find it hard to believe than any person would allow another person to commit the same offense towards them four hundred and ninety times in order to forgive them that much. Conversely, from experience I can remember events that took place once, but lived on hundreds of times in my mind. Even if I had disconnected from the person, isolated myself, or moved on, the memories continued to replay. Even if I had forgiven the person for it and talked through it with them, when I relived the memory and wasn't careful, I would become angry or hurt all over again.

I learned that every time I relived it, I had to forgive all over again.

Learning this lesson, I began helping myself to forgive by not rehearsing the offense repeatedly in my mind. I'm the type of person that wants to talk it out, get to the bottom of it, learn why you did it, and hopefully how we can avoid it in the future. Nevertheless, that is not always possible and other times learning all of those details only made the wound deeper. So I allow myself to embrace the feelings caused by the pain at one time. Whether it takes hours, days, weeks, or months to find relief, I give myself the time needed. When that period is over, I refuse to relive it again.

Refusing to live in past pain frees up your heart to actually heal. As you heal, you can begin the process of forgetting. The mind is a powerful resource and the storage capacity is far beyond what we can understand. The type of forgetting I speak of, is not where you cannot remember any longer. This forgetting is when you make a conscious decision not to allow those negative thoughts to roam free in your mind. This forgetting is keeping your past behind you and not allowing your present to be polluted with the garbage of your yesterdays. It is the same forgetting Paul spoke of when he said, "Forgetting those things which are behind, and reaching forth to the things which are ahead."[6] It is not that he has erased anything from its permanent impression in the corridors of his mind. On the contrary, he was choosing not to be distracted by the memories of his past, both good and bad, because he was so focused on reaching forward.

When you forgive, you make a conscious decision to forget those things which are behind you and put all of your energy into reaching forward to the greater which lies ahead of you.

Harboring unforgiveness in your heart and mind is a willful choice to be stagnated and constantly distracted.

Unforgiveness holds you captive to the date and time the offense took place. It becomes a prison that forces you in a mental box so that you are continuously being faced with the heartache, agitation, and frustration caused by the action of another. While it may also seem that you are punishing the offender, you end up punishing yourself more by repeatedly inflicting pain on the wound initially caused by another. On top of which you become aggravated by giving place for the situation to dwell. The longer unforgiveness sits in your heart, the higher the risk of infection and affection to other areas of your life.

Unforgiveness is the breeding ground for prejudice. Think about what happens within you when someone hurts you significantly. Other people you meet with the same name automatically turn you off. Other people with the same position or title make you apprehensive. You may begin to generalize a whole population of people who are similar in demographics to your offender all because this individual has tarnished your view of everything you perceive them to represent.

It happens all the time. Think about how many people don't trust preachers and prophets and think they're all crooked concerning money and women. Where did that start? It started with someone having a bad experience with an individual, and projecting that stereotype on the entire population. Think about how many people view politicians as crooked, selfish, and self-centered based on the wrongful actions of individuals and not every single politician that exists. Some women become so hurt by their ex-boyfriend or husband that they turn to women because they view all men as the man who hurt them. Likewise some men turn to men because of women who have broken their hearts. Think about how many women are not trusting of other women simply because they had an ignorant woman to cross them.

Is there sometimes a trend in behavior of people with similar demographics? Yes, of course! However, to create a blanket opinion of everyone else who may have some similar traits is a major risk that many of us encounter. Prejudices form when grudges are held in one's heart against another. Although it begins as an ill feeling towards that individual, it festers and can grow into a much larger ill feeling.

HOW CLOSE DO YOU WANT THEM?

When you choose not to forgive you continue to give the offender free access to your heart. Think about how you feel when the person you are upset with walks in the room. If your mood changes, disposition changes, thoughts change, or emotions go into turmoil then it is obvious that person still has power over your heart strings.

Unfortunately, not everyone who offends you is remorseful about it. Some people get a kick out of seeing you squirm. While we are often taught not to allow your enemies to see you sweat, what is more effective than pretending you're not affected is actually not being affected. I am personally not very good at faking how I feel about a person. My husband tells me not to wear my emotions on my sleeve. This I understand when you are in an elevated position and all eyes are watching you. Nonetheless, my emotions on my sleeve isn't a concern when my emotions are not negative. Therefore, what my goal became was changing my emotional response to the presence of people I did not particularly desire to be around. The bottom line was, I had to forgive them.

When Jesus was dying on the cross he said, "Forgive them, for they know not what they do."[7] This seems to be an untrue statement. The soldiers were well aware of what they were doing. They intended to crucify Jesus. They enjoyed mocking him and laughing at his seemingly unfortunate state. They had crucified many others before, and he would not be the last person to die a death on the cross. So what did Jesus really mean?

Jesus was saying, they are ignorant of their own foolishness. While they are trying to hurt me, they are truly hurting themselves. They believe their taunting and actions are killing me, however, I am laying down my own life because of my covenant with my Father. They could never kill me. So Father forgive them, because when this is over and they realize who I am they will become aware of how wrong they truly are.

Sometimes people are doing things to you intentionally because they don't know your true identity. It's amazing how people form their perception of others in today's society. More of what we believe to "know" about a person is based on hearsay and not experience or first-hand information. Think about how many people you've disliked because of something someone else told you about them? Maybe one of your friends had a bad experience with that person and now you don't like them either because of what you heard. You may be rude to them or easily agitated by them because of what you "know." I've literally seen and experienced people wanting to fight others based on lies they were told. They thought… that you thought that you were better… because they said… that you said something about someone else…wow, isn't that confusing?

Oh how many times people have come to me after the fact and said, "I thought you were mean." Or I heard you were judgmental. I heard you said something about me. Then when they actually sit down and get to know me, they find out what they've heard is so far from my character and the truth. Jesus said, forgive them because they think I'm a criminal, but really I'm the complete opposite.

Another great lesson we learn from Jesus on the cross is to forgive as soon as possible. Even as soon as in the midst of the storm forgive them. I've been guilty of wanting to wait until all the dust settled to begin forgiving, but the sooner you choose to forgive the purer you can keep your heart and mind.

When you remain angry with a person they are constantly on your mind. How irritating is that? You don't want to think about them because they bring up negative feelings and thoughts within you. Yet and still you can't escape it because it has become the focal point in your heart. If it is true that "out of the abundance of the heart, the mouth speaks,"[8] then think about the words and conversations you carry on when you're harboring unforgiveness.

SOME THINGS ARE JUST UNFORGIVABLE

We can all think of horrific things that happen in today's world that we feel are simply unforgivable. Murder, rape, molestation, child abuse and neglect, unsolicited violence against defenseless people, stealing, cheating, and the list could go on and on of things you may perceive as unforgiveable. Let me ask you one question. What wrong have you done in your life that you would wave forgiveness benefits from?

While our focus has been on the offender, the sad truth is many people who have trouble forgiving others also have trouble forgiving themselves. Harboring unforgiveness causes residual effects. You may also begin struggling with your own self-perception. Withholding forgiveness from others puts you in a place of condemnation. Yet he that is without sin is the only person worthy of casting the stone of condemnation.

THE HARDEST ONE TO FORGIVE

When you learn to forgive yourself, then you may become more effective forgiving others. If you hold yourself hostage to your mistakes, and less admirable decisions you've made, there is no doubt you will not easily forgive anyone else. When it came down to it, and I really evaluated my heart and life, I realized the one person I struggled forgiving the most was ME.

How could I be so stupid? How could I let that person get so close to me? How could I let that happen? Why didn't I see it sooner? Why didn't I speak up sooner? Why did I let my guard down? Why did I give them another chance to hurt me again? What did I do to deserve their actions towards me? Why didn't I love myself enough to protect myself? What is it about me that attract these kinds of people to me? Why am I so weak? Who is going to want me this broken? Who is going to value me in this state?

The beatings I put myself through are far worse than I could ever inflict on anyone else. I have hurt myself worse than anyone else ever could. All of this stemmed from the fact that I could not forgive myself for making the best choice I knew to make in the moment. I didn't learn till after the moment it was not the best choice. Somehow I still managed to hold myself hostage for what I was ignorant to.

When you know better, just do better. Learning better shouldn't make you go back to beat yourself up for what you decided before you knew. Being a perfectionist caused me to hold myself to unrealistic standards of living. Some things I just had to learn with time and experience, and other things I would learn when I was ready for the challenge of the lesson. Either way I am learning how to look at my mistakes and draw wisdom from them so I can help teach others who show up for life's class.

So by now, you are able to draw your own conclusion. Is choosing not to forgive worth all of the baggage attached to it? Would you rather travel heavy or light in life's journey? Not only does unforgiveness affect your thoughts and emotions, but mental stress affects your body eventually. How much of your well-being are you willing to jeopardize to hold onto a grudge?

People literally have heart attacks, psychological breakdowns, high blood pressure, increased risk for stokes, stomach ulcers, etc. holding on to painful experiences. Because they refuse to release it from their mind and heart, it begins to infiltrate every area of their existence, and subtracts from their quality of life. Are you willing to live life beneath your intended value because you're spending your joy, peace, love, and more to continue possessing unforgiveness? How much anxiety do you want in your life?

Harboring unforgiveness is like leasing a bad car. In the beginning it costs less. It looks good for your image. Perhaps you feel it makes you look strong and powerful. After a while, when it's time to either renew your lease or return the car, you realize you have to pay extra for the additional mileage you've run up on the car you've contracted; and any wear and tear on the car that's significant you are also fined for. All the money and time you've invested in the car thus far is gone. At the end of all those payments it's still not yours.

You think you've been maintaining control of your life and heart by choosing not to forgive. Sadly enough, at the end of all the time you've spent refusing to forgive, you still don't own your own life. You have run up the miles with unnecessary stress, strife, hatred, malice, tension, agitation, aggravation, turmoil, and anger and still have not possessed anything you really wanted to. You thought you were buying your own security, peace, joy, happiness, love, and insurance or assurance plan. In reality you were only getting those things temporarily. At the end of all the lies you were telling yourself, you are left more hurt, more broken, more scarred, more devastated, and more impacted than you ever imagined you would be.

Today you can make the decision to forgive yourself first. Then begin the process of taking an inventory of every person you have not forgiven, and choose to forgive them one by one. Initially it may not feel good, but you will reach the day when you look back and admit, this feels so much better!

5

Breaking the Cycle

So many times in life we repeat the same detrimental cycles multiple times. Many times we do this unintentionally and sometimes completely oblivious to the fact. More times than not we do not make a deliberate decision to repeat the same behaviors we have criticized others for committing. Still, if we are honest with ourselves we have committed some similar deeds and many times not made the correlation.

Everything we think, say, feel, or do comes from an initial seed entering our heart or mind. These seeds enter through our eyes, ears, and experiences. Our eyes take millions of snapshots every single day. Things we see on television, things we see in our homes, communities, and environments are depositing seeds. Think about how you can watch a television show or movie, or see something during the day and dream about it that night. Sometimes we are not even aware of how many seeds have entered through the gates of our eyes.

Our ears also give place for seeds to be planted. What do you hear throughout the course of a day? The radio in the car, music played in public places, conversations you're apart of or overhear, environmental sounds, and any other types of noise. I often laugh at my son Judah when we're in a store at the mall because he's always dancing to the music. Most times I'm so busy concentrating on what I'm looking at that I don't even acknowledge what I'm hearing. Even though I wasn't intentionally listening, it often happens later on in the day or the next day I may be humming a tune I didn't even know I was listening to. Songs I would never listen to on the radio get planted in my ear at the stop light when the next car is blasting their music. We hear so much and it gets planted, whether we want it to be or not.

Experience is a big seed sowing event. Depending on how intense the experience is, good or bad, the impression depth will vary. All experiences plant seeds and help shape your perception of yourself, your life, people, your surroundings, and your world. How we perceive anyone or anything is stemmed from our experiences with knowledge from book learning, life learning, or people learning. Book knowledge, or google knowledge in this day and age, is what we read and study. Life learning is what we learn by exposure, first handedly or second. Second hand life learning is when others share their experiences with us and we learn valued lessons based on their perception of their experience. People learning is simply knowledge we store based on our experiences with people. When we have limited exposure to certain classifications of people we generalize a population based on the few representatives we have seen, whether in person or through media.

As long as you're living, you should be learning. When you stop learning, your life has halted even if your breath has not.

If it's true that all of these areas plant seeds in our hearts and mind, then how do we manage the harvest? Seeds are only productive when they fall into ground and conditions conducive for its fermentation. The right seed, in the right ground, with the right nutrients, and right timing will always yield fruit. What keeps our lives from being overgrown by all the seeds planted every single day through either avenue is how we feed the seed. Notice how memories fade that you do not rehearse, but how vividly you can describe others that you have repeated over and over in your mind.

Jesus spoke a parable about the seed and the different types of grounds it entered[9]. It was the same seed sown into four different soils and but it returned a different results from each one. The ground is our heart. Just like natural seeds, plants, flowers, and greenery only grow and continue to live and be healthy based on the care it's given, so it is with the emotional and mental seeds planted within us. If you don't want a seed to grow into a harvest, or a continued cycle of negativity in your life, you have to be careful not to feed it or let the weeds run wild through negligence.

IDENTIFY THE INITIATING EVENT

Track the earliest event in the chain of reactions that take/took place to find the root of the behavior. By doing this, you will not only gain a better understanding, but may also develop empathy towards the offenders. You may also position yourself to become a significant intersection that redirects people from destructive patterns, to being productive citizens.

I have been so offended by people's behaviors in times past because I only focused on what I could see, or what they were saying, or what their disposition was. How often have you experienced a person with a nasty attitude while you were going to purchase something in a store or restaurant? You walk up to the counter and you're spoken to in a tone, or with words, you were not expecting or appreciative of. If you're not careful, your attitude changes and you attempt to respond to the person with a similar attitude, tone, or choice words. Their demeanor and attitude was the activating event in your heart and mind. I know that it traveled to your mind because as they were speaking, you began thinking to yourself "Who are they talking to?" "What is their problem?" And other questions that then traveled to your heart because as you answered your own questions in your mind, the reality that they were talking to YOU caused your emotions to respond.

That example is a simple one, and common to many of us. But let's go deeper to some more hurtful activating events. What happens when seeds of abuse, infidelity, betrayed trust, usury, thievery, or physical harm are presented to your heart?

I have experienced multiple types of abusive behavior directed towards me, and presented in front of me towards others. I've experienced one of the craziest experiences of my life three times. Once as a child, then twice as an adult I was choked. Each time were with people I love very dearly, and I know love me too. Yet in the heat of those moments our love for each other was nowhere in sight, and I was so stubborn and angry that when I heard the words "I will kill you," I said in my mind, "please do." I was so hurt emotionally to be in that position that I couldn't feel anything physically being done to me. After the adrenaline subsided then the soreness came and so did the resentment. Leaving with concussions from being hit in the head, weeks of headaches to follow. Each time that experience it was a more severe burn to my heart. My heart was completely closed and I felt it would never be opened again.

How do you move on from something as traumatic as that? Not easily at all! These were not strangers on the street, but people I would be connected to forever.

In the winter of 2000 my mother and I had a disagreement. I can only tell this today because her and I have resolved this matter, and moved on from this event that occurred many years ago in my childhood. It was a Sunday afternoon and I'd just come home from being at my dad's house that weekend. It snowed the day prior, so there was snow and ice on the sidewalks. My mother sent me to the corner store to get a few items. I can admit, I was not excited to go to the store because I didn't feel like falling and slipping on the icy path to the store. I don't mind snow, but I detest walking in dirty snow and ice. I went to the store, got what she told me, and came back. I took the bags to the kitchen and proceeded to go back to my room. This was not a good period of time in my relationship with my mother. I tried to just stay to myself to avoid getting in trouble so often.

My mom was on the phone with someone, I believe one of my aunts. She went looking in the bags and apparently didn't find something she was looking for. She called me back downstairs to tell me I'd forgotten something from her list. I disagreed. I knew I got everything she said, she must've forgot to tell me. So she sent me back to the store. By this time I was really getting a bad attitude. Apparently she was as well because when I came back she addressed my attitude. I don't remember everything that was said, but I remember going upstairs to my room. Knowing myself, I was probably mumbling something on the way upstairs. All I remember is she was in my room with me and she was HEATED.

I've always been respectful to my mother, in the sense that I would never raise my hands to her, but I was not afraid of her. As she fussed and ranted I just looked at her waiting for her to shut up. Then she got up in my face yelling at me. I stood there and took it. I figured I'd just let her get it all out and then lay down when she left my room and listen to the radio. She lifted her hand, I thought to hit me in my face, but she says she wasn't trying to hit me but basically about to point in my face. I lifted my hand to block my face and my mom saw red. She thought I was trying to fight her. So she proceeded to teach me what being in a fight with her would feel like. She punched me multiple times, and I just got tired. I tried to hold her hands and she got that mother strength that only comes when a mother feels threatened by a child, and she pinned me on my bed. She got on top of me and before she knew it her hands were around my throat.

All I could do was look up at her. I looked her straight in her eyes. She didn't even look like my mother in that moment. We were not mother and daughter, we were enemies. I didn't try to remove her hands from my neck. I didn't try to grab at her arms. I was content with letting her choke the life out of me. Obviously, she did not because I'm here writing about it today. Something snapped in her mind and brought her back to reality and she released me, got off of me, and went back downstairs. I remember lying there in the same position for a while and I just cried.

Ironically, I didn't cry because I was hurt by the event. I cried because I wasn't sure if it was better to survive or die. If I had died, all of my pain would end. Since I was still alive, the possibility that this could happen again remained.

What I remember about that time in my childhood that was significantly enlightening, was when I spoke to my grandmother on the phone, begging for someone to come get me. My grandmother, Diana, asked me if I wanted her to come over, and I said yes. I could tell she was surprised at my response, but I wanted her there to see my face, see my hurt, and see my heart. She came to my bedroom and held me on my bed. I cried in her arms. Then I asked her, why I couldn't come live with her. All my other cousins had lived with my grandparents at one time or another, except me. I didn't think it was fair. She said to me, "My mother did the same thing to me when I was young. And I probably did the same thing to your mother. You will get through this."

Then I realized that my mother didn't begin the cycle, but I definitely was going to break it! From that day on I never allowed people to play with me like they were choking me. I can't stand people touching my neck. I don't like people in my personal space that I don't know, and I prefer not to be touched by people in certain settings. My mother and I did not get along for many years to follow. I was emotionally detached from her until I left for the army after high school graduation. It wasn't until I was gone from home for three years that I even explained to her how much that incident impacted my perception of her. While we are not "best friends," we have a healthy relationship and she is a great grandmother to my children.

I could have left home and left her altogether, but I didn't. I took care of her financially when she was struggling with health issues and unemployment. Even when I was bitter, because she is my mother, I had to honor her. This was a situation that I couldn't escape. I had to learn how to work through it. My perception of the situation changed when I realized she was raising me the way she was raised. She felt like we were fighting, but I never raised my hands to hit her. I raised my hands to protect my face from being hit, but her perception and mine were completely different.

Domestic violence was another pattern. I saw my grandparents fight. I saw my parents fight. And then I would repeat the same cycle and fight too. Knowing how horrible it was, yet without making any attempt the cycle lived on. If you try to disconnect from the reality of your family's cycles, you will likely repeat them because you have not actively gone after them. Cycles only break with conscious efforts.

IDENTIFY THE FIRST EVENT YOU CAN CONTROL

Some things you just can't control, and that's okay. We are not responsible for anyone's initial interaction with us. Yet, as we respond and react then we can affect how others respond and react to us. Find the initial point where you can begin to influence the cycle in a different direction.

As you identify that, you can prepare yourself not to always be reactive, but be proactive most of the time.

You cannot control how people talk to you initially, just like I couldn't control the anger in others that caused me physical, emotional, or mental harm. One of the biggest lessons I had to learn was how to let go of what I could not control. I accepted that I cannot control people, the choices they make, or the thought patterns that lead to those choices. When a person intersects with me in my life I can only control my response to the situation presented.

I've been the fool and am learning to be wiser, but life has a tendency of bringing you back to the lessons you have not learned, and tests you have not passed. Like my mother, I used to be a real hot head. My cousins can attest to how I fought as a child, mainly in my junior high school years. I fought girls, boys, whoever. Some were my size and age, others were bigger, but all did something to push my buttons. I didn't have any fear of getting hurt, which I thought was good because I wasn't afraid of anyone. The foolish side of that is some people need to be feared, especially those who don't value anyone else's life but their own. I didn't think about the fact they could kill me and go take a nap.

I grew up in South Philadelphia and I had to be tough. I saw plenty of fights in my day. I come from a family who believed in fighting for and with one another. If you messed with one of us, we wouldn't jump you, but we would fight you until one of us won. We fought people who came with bats and knives, and we used our hands to defend ourselves and make it so you wouldn't try us again. While I was walking into church one day I saw a person shot and killed point blank range. I've had to run in the house while people were outside having a shootout in the middle of the afternoon. I never went looking for fights, but I had a low tolerance for being "disrespected."

When I left Philadelphia and joined the army at age eighteen, I was in for a rude awakening. Basic training was my first experience where I had to learn how to hold my peace against some prejudice and trifling remarks from people who only said things because they knew no one wanted to get in trouble for fighting. That was the beginning of my learning how to prioritize what really mattered, my pride or my success. Back then I was only a private in the Army, the lowest rank possible. It didn't seem I had much to lose. It was the beginning of my career and how I learned self-control would influence the pace at which I excelled above my peers.

Another big cultural shock for me was southern church women. I can laugh about it even as I type because I've seen and experienced things in the South at churches that I know wouldn't have flown in Philadelphia. I've been bumped, cursed at, harassed, called every name in the book of insults, and felt disrespected even while being pregnant. The two things that kept me from resorting back to my basic instincts were my military clearance and my Holy Spirit. I often joke to myself and say, "Jesus is saving more people than they realize on today."

I had to learn how to keep people from pushing my buttons, or even having access to my buttons. I have absolutely no control over how people initiate an experience or encounter with me. I can only control how I respond and either agitate the situation, or extinguish it. I would be a liar if I said I always felt like extinguishing things. Sometimes my natural side wants to show people who they're messing with, and teach them a lesson. Sometimes I want to be "the one" to help change the way some people freely disrespect others they don't know. But at what cost? I'm not willing to jeopardize my success and wellbeing for people who have less to lose, and nothing to gain.

In the process of writing this book I had a heart check. I found myself having to fully release some people who had taunted me for years. As I was in the midst of having my heart cleansed, I heard very clearly "release them." In that moment I took out my phone and sent a message to two individuals I've wanted to have physical altercations with. People who had been so disrespectful to my face, and more so behind my back. People who constantly sought to bring confusion and chaos to my life. People I had a right disliked. I simply said, "Whether you feel you need it or not, I want you to know I forgive you for everything you've done intentionally and unintentionally to me. I pray that you find true happiness and joy in your life and within your family."

My heart sank as I sent those words, because these people would never apologize to me. Even in sending it, that gives me no guarantee they'll stop doing what they've been doing. In my mind I tried to resist this and say I could forgive without contacting them; or that I should wait until they contacted me for forgiveness and then tell them. I just wanted to leave it alone. Surprisingly, this was not about them at all! It was solely about the condition of my heart.

When your heart's purity becomes more important than your pride, you are ready to break the cycle.

I am at peace with not having control over anyone else's actions but my own. That peace allows me to make wiser decisions that keep me in character, even when my emotions would lead me out of character. This doesn't happen overnight, and is not an easy pill to swallow. Yet if you're honest with yourself, you can look back on some decisions you've made and admit your response wasn't worth the aftermath. Some people thrive off of agitating others as a form of entertainment, probably because they are not busy enough working on improving their own lives.

Another thing that motivates this mindset is knowing that every word I speak, or action I commit goes down in history forever. I'm trying to live my life in a way that when others read my story, I don't have to be ashamed of much. I often think, if I ended up on the news or in the public's eye for my reaction, would I be more ashamed or content with that publicity? Celebrities and other public figures don't get many opportunities to have private blow-ups. Everything negative they do we see broadcasted. While I'm not a celebrity, I am an example to those who are around me. I have influence on some people intentionally, and many times unintentionally on people I did not even realize were watching me. I know for a fact there were days if I would've jumped to fight, I had several other women who would've jumped to fight too. But because I held my peace, they were shown how to hold theirs too.

I refuse to be led by bad leadership. When bad leaders arise, I chose to stop following and become a leader.

If you're ever going to break the cycle, you have to make up in your mind that you're not going to follow the bad leader. Often times we don't view the offender as a leader, but a leader is anyone who has influence over another person to the point of influencing their mindset or behavior. If you are always responding to offenders, then you are allowing them to influence your mindset and behavior in the direction they've initiated. However, when you identify their action, and the course of reactions that could take place, you can then choose to take away their leading authority by going in a different direction with your response.

PREPARE YOUR NEW RESPONSE

Because we know that we will inevitably be offended in the future by someone, somewhere, for some reason be wise enough to mentally prepare, and prevent having to think on your feet when you are emotionally shaken by predictable situations. We are unable to force others to change, but we can change ourselves.

No one's actions change permanently without their mind changing first.

In the beginning of breaking certain cycles, I was just pretending not to be bothered by situations. I would psyche myself out, trying to talk myself into thinking that I wasn't really offended for various reasons. I would say stuff like, "they're beneath me," "they're not on my level," "they're so miserable being them, they're trying to be me." I mean, I would go on and on, feeding my ego so I could numb the pain of being offended, hurt, disappointed, sad, and angry, etc. That only worked for so long, and it only led me to implode.

Psyching yourself out is simply deceiving yourself. The worse person to deceive in this life is your own self! I realized I had to find a better way or I would end up snapping one day and God only knew what I would do with all that built up tension, frustration, anger, malice, hatred, agitation, confusion, bitterness, and darkness. So I stopped psyching myself out, and learned how to prepare for a new response that was genuine to how I felt.

After I made peace with not being able to control anyone else's behaviors, and decided that I would not follow bad leadership, then I determined who I wanted to be in the fabric of my heart. I decided that I wanted to be a loving, compassionate, peaceful, joy filled, forgiving, and gentle person. I wanted to have the fruit of the Spirit evident in my heart and life: love, joy, peace, long-suffering, kindness, goodness, faithfulness, and self-control[10]. In order to do this, I had to prepare for a new response.

So I started to prepare for situations that had repeatedly occurred in my life. I began coaching myself in how to control myself when faced with people who obviously had no control over themselves. It just didn't make sense for me to allow someone who could not control their own actions, to have control over mine. How could I allow others to make me into a puppet on strings who didn't even control their own strings?

I also started exploring why people behaved in certain manners that seemed to be directed against me. There were some hard truths I had to accept some people are: self-centered, wounded, warring, and/or miserable.

SELF-CENTERED

The first truth is some people are self-centered. Everyone isn't thinking about you when they make their decisions. Some are only thinking of themselves, and not the affects it has on anyone else. You would think that when people pursue adulterous relationships, they would think about how the other spouse and children could be negatively affected by their actions. Sadly enough, the other spouse and children are not in the thought process when making those decisions. Those thoughts are strictly on how they feel, what they're getting, and what's working for them. They don't think about the children and spouse until they get caught and are put in a place where they could lose everything.

Self-centered people are not out to hurt you, they are out to help themselves. Don't take it personal.

These people are not coming up with schemes and plans to do you harm. It is their full intention to make themselves feel better by all means necessary. You are likely hurt by the mere fact they have neglected you in their thinking. It's not that they've spent so much time thinking of ways to hurt you as much as it's through their negligence you were hurt. Many of these people are not out to maliciously hurt anyone, but hurt so many by having tunnel vision smaller than those within their inner circle.

WOUNDED

The second truth is some people are wounded. I've often heard people say, "hurt people, hurt people." It has been proven true in my life. People who are hurt, typically cause more hurt to others. Sometimes these people do it intentionally out of the bitterness of being hurt. Other times people hurt others unintentionally by repeating the cycles they are not healed from themselves. Oh how many times I've seen people become the very thing they hated to see. I've watched women who were cheated on and dogged, become the "other woman." I've seen people who were molested, molest others. I've seen people who were abused, become the abusers. I've seen people who lost loved ones to drugs and alcohol become addicts. I've seen people who were abandoned, abandon their children and families. I've seen people who were robbed become thieves.

Wounded people are contagious people, if you get too close they'll pass their infection to you!

Think about when people have a cold, or upper respiratory infection. People who are in close proximity are at increased risk of catching their cold. It's not because the person wants to get everyone else sick, but sometimes it's because they are not proactive in isolating themselves long enough to get better first. If they cough or sneeze, or rub their nose and touch something that you touch afterwards, when you rub your eyes, nose, or place something in your mouth their infection gets introduced to your body. In a few days, you will start to feel ill as your body's immune system begins fighting against it.

WARRING

Everyone is not out to get you, sometimes you're a casualty of their warfare.

The third truth is some people are warring. War is an ugly thing that exists today. In ancient days, the armies left their homelands and met in neutral grounds to fight. In this way, less women and children were affected by the warfare until the battle was over and one kingdom conquered another. Today's warfare doesn't happen that way. Innocent bystanders are often victims of two opposing forces warring. While I wish we lived in a world where innocent people were not killed or wounded in warfare, we don't. And just like it happens physically, it happens emotionally on a daily basis.

I've known people who truly loved me and cared for me, but I met them or was close to them in the midst of internal warfare, and found myself a casualty of their warfare. While I wished I was excluded, the reality is I was not. So I found myself being hurt, not because of my actions, but by proximity to the person in battle. It was difficult for me to understand how they could be so careless with my heart when they cared so much for me. When we're in the heat of battle we are not always able to control the damage that occurs.

If you've ever tried to break up a fight, you know that you are probably going to get hit. You know that before you go in to break up the fighting people, but you go in anyway because you perceive something worse will happen to one of the people fighting if you don't. You may get hit by the person whose side you're on. You may get hit by the other person. You may get hit by both of them. Neither is aiming to hit you, but you just stepped in the way.

Emotionally we can just step in the way sometimes and get beat up from both sides. Just remember that you saw the battlefield before you tried to intervene. This occurs most often to people who have a hero complex, or a helping heart. Be careful of putting yourself in harm's way if you're not willing to deal with the risk of being hurt yourself.

MISERABLE

The fourth truth is some people are miserable. There's an old saying that "misery loves company." Sometimes people are so unhappy with their own lives that they are okay with jeopardizing your happiness for the chance of feeling better themselves. Sometimes people are bitter, and in their minds feel you don't deserve the joy, happiness, or things you appear to have. While this is an unfortunate person to encounter, they do exist. In these situations, I've learned to avoid helping them achieve their goal.

I refuse to give miserable people my company.

When I encounter people who are always negative about any and everything, I distance myself from them. They could be family, coworkers, church members, whoever! I minimize how often I talk to them, spend time around them, and interact with them. I just refuse to give miserable people my company.

Miserable people that have set themselves as enemies, agitators, or adversaries to me, I ignore. These are not people who can be reasoned with, talked to, or negotiated with. Sometimes the best way to respond is to COMPLETELY IGNORE these people.

I remember a situation where I had a person calling my phone back to back for hours. I couldn't believe they had that much time on their hands to keep calling my phone. I literally had hundreds of calls in one night with maybe six voicemails. Initially I turned my ringer off, after a while I turned my phone off that night. As long as I was texting back, talking back, and being responsive, they just kept repeating the cycles over and over. Eventually, even though I was severely agitated, I learned how to ignore them. Once it finally clicked that I wasn't going to play their game, they stopped.

After I identified these four truths about people, I learned to respond according to the type of person I was dealing with. Self-centered people respond best to communication that makes them put themselves in your shoes. Questions like, "how would you feel if I did that to you?" Wounded people need support in getting help, usually you're not the person to help them, but in some cases you can. Warring people need distance to finish their fight. Miserable people need good distractions. They need something positive to focus on in their own lives to distract them from feeling you don't deserve what you have.

Not everyone will fall in these categories, some people are just immature. They make decisions based on their immature experiences in life, and others are affected. Some people are just ignorant. They really haven't been taught better, had better examples, or sought better enlightenment or instructions. Other people are just insensitive. Sometimes they've had a hard time and their emotions grew callouses and become tough, and they feel everyone else should do the same. Other times they really just don't understand how you feel, and lack the empathy and sympathy to care.

No matter which type of person you find yourself faced with, the bigger question is what type of person are you? Remaining consistent and true to yourself, your identity, your character, and your disposition despite the opposition you face must be your focus if you're going to succeed at breaking the cycle.

COMMIT TO YOUR RESOLUTION

Commitment is one of the essential pieces to success in any area of life. Being able to remain consistent in your change will take a determination that's not easily broken if it's ever going to work. You will not always feel like being the "bigger person." You will not always feel like turning the other cheek. You will not always feel like biting your tongue. You will not always feel like giving up your "right" to be right. Sometimes you will feel like getting even. Sometimes you will feel like getting revenge. Sometimes you will feel like telling people off. Sometimes you will feel like doing bodily harm to people. Sometimes you will feel like causing pain back in their lives. Sometimes you will want to make an example out of someone. Sometimes you will want to defend yourself. Sometimes you will want to use the "I'm only human" card.

I cannot lie to you. This is not going to fix the flood of emotions you have as a human being, but after the floods rage, when the waves calm back down you have to make a decision. Commitments are kept one decision at a time. At each intersection you enter with another person, you must choose which way you want to go. It's really just that simple. The not so simple part is convincing your ego that choosing to walk away, or not engage in tit for tat is better for you.

When my pride or ego is bruised by my commitment to be different, it is often soothed by the peace I live in not worrying about reaping what I've sown. Life becomes so much more peaceful when you don't have to look over your shoulder for people retaliating on you for what you've done to them. Anger and rage are temporary emotions, but peace and calm are meant to be long acting conditions. I choose to live in peace. I can't make myself an enemy to anyone. The only enemies I have are people who have set themselves as enemies to me.

At some point in your life you have to start living for you! Your mindset much change to the degree that every conversation you engage in, every action you perform is all done in efforts to achieve one purpose. When you have a clear purpose and vision for your life before you, nothing anyone else does can effectively distract you or throw you off course. Achieving your purpose and goals must become more important than getting even with anyone else. Staying the course to greatness has to be so valuable that you're willing to forfeit foolishness in order to get there.

When all else fails, know your worth. You are worth your change.

LaChish Latimer

6

I've Got the Power

I'VE GOT THE POWER

How does pain get transformed into personal power? The difference between pain and personal power is perspective. What do you perceive about your life's experiences? How do you view the adversity you've faced? How do you process the hurtful encounters you've had in this life?

In high school I was going through a very challenging time in my relationship with my mother. I had a very close friend who was one of the "star" runners for both cross-country and track. She'd been running in clubs since she was very young. She was good! She was a year younger than me, and we grew very close. We called each other sister. People even thought we looked alike. I guess it was our size and complexion. She and I pushed each other in practices and I followed behind her in races. We built our friendship around running.

One day she came to school and I was in the basement looking at our team's announcement board for the new schedule. She was very calm. She looked at me and said, "My mom died." I couldn't register what she had just said. She was too calm to have said her mother was dead. I remember asking for further explanation. Did she mean literally dead or figuratively? As it turned out, her mother overdosed and died. I was so concerned for her. Where would she live? Who would take care of her and her siblings?

I was as supportive as I knew how to be. I had no idea what to say, or not say. I went to the funeral. I called and checked on her. After things settled down and everyone stopped giving her so much sympathy attention, I remember asking her how she was really doing. Her answer would stun me to no end. She said, "LaChish, I don't know if I should say this? I don't know if it's right to feel this way or not. But I actually feel relieved that my mom is gone. Like it's finally over." My heart sank, how could losing a mother be relieving? That's for most people one of the most devastating experiences in life. For my friend it was different. Her experience with her mother had been negative, stressful, sometimes abusive, often times embarrassing, and apparently overwhelming. She was relieved because she didn't have to come up with any more lies to explain her mother's poor behavior. She would now have an actual caregiver to look after her and her siblings. She could take off the weight of trying to raise them in her mother's place. She'd been living in a nightmare, and felt like she was finally waking up.

Today her perception may be very different. Yet I respected her strength as a fifteen/sixteen year old facing a crisis. She could've collapsed under the pressure of grief and tragedy. Instead she chose to see the positive in the midst of her storm. Death has brought a definite end to an ongoing secret misery. There I was feeling like my relationship with my mother was the worse! We'd never shared our secret stresses of going home. But now she was liberated to tell the truth, and her truth helped change my perspective of my truth. We were both suffering from the disappointment of what a mother-daughter relationship should be. Our ends were drastically different. Her storm would seemingly end, while I would have to outlive mine. Undoubtedly, we are both better mothers because of what we experienced as children.

I have learned to see the lesson in every experience I have. In life, some lessons are just easy. Those lessons are easily forgotten. Yet the lessons that brought tears out of my eyes and pain to my heart are the ones I'll never forget. As I pass each test, it qualifies me to teach others how to pass. As I overcome each obstacle, it qualifies me to coach others to overcome. As I fail a test, it qualifies me to become a detour sign for others not to take that path.

Whether I excel by succeeding, or excel by the process of eliminating what not to do, I'm not ashamed of what I've experienced. My experiences empower me by giving me knowledge. My knowledge is then tamed into wisdom. My wisdom is then shared to become edification. As I edify others, I cause the world around me to be better. As the world around me becomes better, the environment is cleansed of negativity.

By this point in your reading I hope you have begun your own internal restoration process. Often times people pursue healing because it takes away the immediate pain and discomfort. Please don't stop at being healed, you must be made whole. The difference between being healed and being whole is when you heal, there is a lasting awareness or scar, that shows you were once broken. When you are made whole no one can see where you were broken, it is only visible when you open your mouth to share it. Even when you tell others, they have trouble believing you because you truly don't look like what you've been through.

I took the opportunity to read a very profound book one day, entitled "As A Man Thinketh," by James Allen. I came across the book while I was preparing a sermon entitled "I Think I Can!" This book challenged the way I was thinking. It shook the very foundations of my thought processes. It encouraged me to regain control over the course of my life. So many times we are waiting for someone else to rescue us, right the wrongs, or uplift us. The true power is in understanding that within you lies everything you need to change the entire course of your existence.

Life doesn't happen to me, it happens for me.

Three things will show you how your power is used: thoughts, words, and deeds. This entire book has been gauged to expand your thoughts when it comes to interpreting pain. As your thoughts change, so will your words.

Your words will frame your world, but your thoughts will frame you!

When you take hold of the steering wheel in your mind, your life's direction will change. Thoughts are so powerful because these are the words you say to yourself in private. The thoughts you believe are the ones you put into action. Your thoughts are the loudest voice in your life. No one speaks louder than the voice in your mind. It doesn't matter what others say, ultimately you are going to follow what your thoughts say. Direct your thoughts in places you want to go, and watch your life align itself and arrive at that very place.

Pain is used as a speed bump. It may cause you to slow down and take precaution, but it shouldn't completely stop you. Pain is an instrument to challenge your will and test how badly you really want something. Pain is sometimes the purifying agent needed to snap us back into reality.

Pain is a fuel. Either you place it in your tank and drive, or you put a match to it and allow everything to be destroyed.

I use my pain as fuel to be better. I learn from an offense, how not to offend. I have determination deep within me that thrives in the face of opposition. In Exodus chapter one it says that as the taskmasters increased the hardship on the Children of Israel they multiplied greatly. Everyone is not mentally prepared for hardship, but there is a special breed of people that learn how to be even more productive under pressure. I had to learn early in life that life is not a bed of roses, I'd have to learn how to make a garden in the desert.

I'm not the only person who will ever have to suffer, and truth be told, my suffering is minuscule compared to some people who are really suffering in hopeless conditions. The people we look at in amazement, and in awe of their courage and tenacity, are people just like you and I who have made the decision to be empowered by our trials and not deflated.

Pity parties are not for the mentally strong. The moment you allow yourself to slip into feeling sorry for your calamities is the moment you allow yourself to be weakened by the pain and not strengthened.

It is perfectly fine to deal with the emotions and embrace the truth of how you feel, but after that you have to decide to grow from it, in it, and through it. In difficult times you have to determine if you're going to lift the weight and get bigger muscles, or let it crush your neck and kill you. I'm choosing the bigger, more defined muscles option.

My life has not been easy. God knows there were many times I wanted to quit and throw in the towel, but He just wouldn't let me do it. By the time I turned sixteen I felt I had suffered enough in my life that I didn't need to suffer anymore to learn. I wanted every lesson from then on to be learned through reading, or listening to other's experiences. Needless to say, since then I've experienced more hardships and challenges than I "signed up for." Even when I tried my hardest to do things the right way, I still felt like I was reaping bad harvests.

I memorized "And let us not be weary in well doing, for in due season we shall reap, if we faint not.[11]" I can't tell you how many days and situations I had to keep repeating this to myself in order to hold on. I've been to my breaking point and wanted to quit on life altogether. I've attempted suicide multiple times as a child and even as an adult, but the purpose God placed in me refused to die. I am not writing from something I've heard, or read, or something I am a novice in. I'm writing from experience. I know what pain feels like.

I've suffered emotional pain. I've suffered physical ailments that were painful. I've suffered mental pain and battled depression. I've suffered spiritual pain, and felt my spirit was broken. My will and drive were broken. Yet, I encourage others that no matter what pain you've experienced, you can turn it into personal power.

The power is personal because it is a strength that exudes from the inside out. It is a mental fortitude that causes you to be resilient against any adversity you'll face in life. I embrace adversity because it shows me what I'm really made of. I embrace hardships and have learned how to endure so that even when what was meant for bad, must turn out for good.

Joseph said to his brother, "what you meant for evil, God has transformed for good.[12]" I know that not everyone believes in my dreams. I know not everyone is cheering for me in this game of life. Yet I choose to believe that the only way all things work together for my good is when I perceive them in a constructive way. Even when evil is pursued against me, it will turn out for my good because I will become a better person in the process.

FOUR POWERS

Knowing what pain feels like, let's now exercise the power we've been given as well. There are four main powers we are given: el, exousia, yad, and dynamis.

EL: This is a Hebrew word for power that denotes a god-like power, mighty in strength, mighty things in nature, extraordinary strength. It is often times used to describe heroic people who do great things with their physical body. It is the type of power seen when mothers lift cars off of their children, or men run into rescue victims and have supernatural strength to lift things that are normally too heavy.

Sometimes the cares of life can be overwhelming and seem too heavy to lift. When you look at the various situations before you, it may seem impossible to recover from the weight of heaviness life has laid on you. Yet there is a power available to you that causes the unbearable burden to be carried. All odds may be stacked against you, but you have a mighty power within you because your Father has made you in His image and likeness.

EXOUSIA: This is a Greek word for power that denotes a power of choice. It is expressed as the liberty one possesses to do what pleases them. It is also a power of authority through influence and of right through privilege. It is the power to rule over and take jurisdiction over.

When life seems out of control, this is the power you must pull on to bring things back together. You have been given power over the jurisdiction of your mind. You are to rule over, watch over, regulate, and control the realm of your thoughts. You have the power over the atmosphere of your home. You have the authority over your flesh. You must exert your authority to bring your thoughts, emotions, words, and actions into alignment with your successfulness. If you don't rule yourself, you will be ruled by the influence of others.

YAD: This is a Hebrew word for power that portrays the ability to shape or control by way of authority. It is illustrated like the power in a hand that manipulates, moves, maneuvers, and manages what it touches. This is the power given to the words you speak out to either produce life or death. This is a sensitive source of power that does not limit the fruit of what's spoken only to pleasantries, but brings forth both good and bad.

You will have what you say. Yad encourages us to say what we truly desire, and refrain from speaking negatively. This is vitally crucial in your transformation because you cannot continue to speak according to where you are and what you feel in the moment. You have to use the power of your words to shape the life you want to see. The more you speak positively to yourself and your surroundings, the quicker your mindset will believe for better. When your mind locks in and agrees with your words, your actions are bound to follow in pursuing the path to greater. You have the power to speak yourself out of the rut you're in.

DYNAMIS: This is a Greek word for power that is referred to as a gift from God to perform the miraculous. It is the power that emanates from the spirit. It is not an emotional power. It is not a mental power. It is not a physical power. It is according to Strong's Concordance "inherent power, power residing in a thing by virtue of its nature, or which a person or thing exerts and puts forth."

This is the power that makes all things possible! This power is used to bring healing to the broken. This power is used to enlighten and free the bound mind. This power is used to bring love back to a heart stained by hatred and resentment. This power is used to bring hope back to a hopeless. This power is used to bring faith back to a fearful.

This power extends beyond the walls of intellect, and makes achievable that which cannot be naturally figured out. It does not often give full clarity to our psychological faculties. It makes you say things like, "I don't know how I got over it, but I am." It brings about a peace that cannot be explained. It brings a calm that seems irrational and even inappropriate compared to your painful experience. This is the power of God working in man's affairs.

KNOWLEDGE IS POWER

When I consider the myriad of experiences and encounters I've had in this life, I realize how much more I know because of it. I never would know how to overcome the challenge of being pained if I never went through any pain myself. Trying to encourage others in their time of need becomes so much easier when you've experienced similar emotions, even if the circumstances are far different.

Before I got married I was anxious to get out of the single life. I always knew I wanted to be a mother. I wanted to be a great wife too. I always felt I was a great girlfriend, always supportive of my mate. I was a great friend to them. I was a great cheerleader. I was committed. One thing the Army helped further instill in me was the value of integrity and commitment. While my husband and I dated I was privileged to be a great friend and support for him during one of the hardest times of his life. He often tells me he never expected me to be there through the width and breadth of his storm. For me, it was never an option not to at least be a great friend for him. Even if the romantic side weakened, I would never leave him to suffer alone.

After that season ended we got married. He actually cried during the vows, reflecting on how beautiful the wedding day was after so many gloomy days over the last couple of years. I thought to myself, "Yes! The pain is over!" I mean, after having gone through so much dating I just knew marriage would be a bed of roses.

Fortunately, it was not the picture perfect experience I was looking for. Yes I said fortunately. We have learned so many insightful things through our ignorance and mistakes. I now understand that some things I had to go through to learn. David said it was good that he was afflicted because it caused him learn God's statutes[13]. It was good for me to be afflicted in every area of my life, so that I could learn lessons and wisdom others would expect, demand, and request from me.

The pain of affliction has been my professor in life.

In school, it's common for the professor who seems the hardest to be the student's least favorite. Yet many times that same professor's course is the one students remember more from than the easier courses. Pain may not be your favorite professor, but it is the one you learn so much from. Like any other school, it's important you take all the courses and not just one. Finding the balance between learning from pain, and being crippled by what pain has exposed is crucial.

GETTING STRONGER

Muscle failure is part of any physical fitness regimen when strength training is the goal. During a muscle failure session, a specific muscle group is targeted and worked out until it cannot go any further. In true muscle failure the aim is to exercise that isolated muscle over and over until it is completely fatigued. That means that you have used all its strength in that session. Of course balancing muscle failure with muscle injury is important, but you want to work out until that muscle feels weak. You must perform the exercise repeatedly until you cannot successfully complete another repetition.

The day after muscle failure sessions are usually uncomfortable. You are really sore and often stiff. You feel like you never want to do that session again. The effects linger on for a day or few days after the event is over. You have literally ripped your muscles, and now they must heal. The ripping is not a complete separation, but causes micro tears in the muscle fibers. These microscopic tears heal, but when they heal the muscle has become a little bigger. Not only has it become a little bigger, but it has also become a little stronger. Each time a muscle failure session is complete the next time you enter the session you are stronger.

After consistent training, you will find it takes more repetitions to reach muscle failure. Your endurance has increased. What once was difficult and nearly impossible is now a "light day." When you take a day to assess your progress is when you fully understand what all that pain was about. You are stronger and you look even better.

Life's painful experiences will often times put us in emotional or mental failure. While some people completely collapse, have mental breakdowns, quit, become suicidal or homicidal, there is a point of failure that produces stronger emotional and mental beings. I'm a firm believer that we are not given more than we can bear in this life. We are, however, given more than we want to bear often times. Have confidence that no matter how fatiguing your experiences may seem, once you make it out of this "session" you will be stronger than you ever expected.

The only way muscle failure becomes productive physically is if you don't quit when it gets uncomfortable. Likewise, if you try to emotionally and mentally check out when life gets uncomfortable you will forfeit the benefits that accompany the hardship. True mental health is not people who do not have any negative thoughts or emotions. True mental health is the person who has the mental fortitude to stand in the midst of an emotional storm and not give up. Tears may run down your face, but you don't give up. Chest pains may hurt your heart, but you don't give up. Fear may try to transform your thinking, but you don't give up. You must get to the place that you keep on pushing until you just can't push anymore. By that time, your storm will be over, and you will enter recovery phase.

Recovery phase is the times in life when you are not emotionally challenged. These are the peaceful, joyful, happy times. Enjoy these times to the fullest! Don't waste time in recovery worrying about the next dreadful turmoil. Enjoy getting stronger and defining your emotional and mental muscles. You may start out without any emotional stamina or agility, but if you are willing to embrace the positive side of pain, you will arise as a powerful resource in the lives of those you influence.

CONCLUSION

Pain is a source of discouragement in the pursuit of victory. When we meet pain, it is a battle of our will against the will of pain. Only one side can win. Although the battle may render wounds to both parties, when the battle is over there will arise a victor. At times pain is sent to try to discourage, dishearten, and dismantle us. Pain does not have a guaranteed victory and the outcome is determined by you.

But pain is not always our enemy. Pain is an indicator that you're still alive. When my patients wake up from their anesthetic from surgery and feel pain, they know they didn't die on the table. Pain is also indicative of new life. Whether labor pains that signal the soon coming birth of a child, or the growth of a new tooth, or the growth of bigger muscles.

Pain is a check on learning. It is a keen awareness that we must choose wisely in this life. It is our teacher, instructor, and motivation to not remain a fool. It is a fine tuner of individual character and provokes maturity.

I have made my choice. I know how I will respond to pain. I will become more patient. I will become more loving. I will become more temperate. I will become more kind. I will become gentler. I will become more understanding. I will become wiser. I will become more determined. I will become more passionate. I will become more pure. I will become more positive. I will become more skilled. I will become stronger. I will become more vigilant.

I refuse to face any adversity, hardship, or painful infliction without leaving it better. Jacob wrestled with the Angel and refused to let go until he was blessed. Although, he left with a hip that was bruised and a painful limp that followed. He also left with a new identity and the blessing of favor on his life[14].

We will all be dealt our share of pain in this life. What will separate you from others is how you choose to accept and adapt to your afflictions.

Today's struggle can be tomorrow's source of strength if I choose to perceive it so tonight.

My final challenge to you is very simple. If you have indeed found the content of this book to be helpful in your personal development, healing, and advancement then share it with one person you believe would benefit from it. Pass it forward! One by one, we will heal our generation and improve our world.

REFERENCES

Scripture quotations are from The King James Version

1. Jeremiah 17:9
2. Luke 7:47
3. Matthew 6:15
4. Romans 12:19b
5. Matthew 18:21-22
6. Philippians 3:13b
7. Luke 23:34
8. Matthew 12:34
9. Matthew 13
10. Galatians 5:22-23
11. Galatians 6:9
12. Genesis 50:20
13. Psalm 119:71
14. Genesis 32:22-31